Pagan Portals

Sacred Landscape: Caves & Mountains

A multi-Path exploration of the
world around us

Pagan Portals

Sacred Landscape: Caves & Mountains

A multi-Path exploration of the world around us

Mélusine Draco

MOON BOOKS

Winchester, UK
Washington, USA

JOHN HUNT PUBLISHING

First published by Moon Books, 2020
Moon Books is an imprint of John Hunt Publishing Ltd., No. 3 East Street, Alresford
Hampshire SO24 9EE, UK
office@jhpbooks.net
www.johnhuntpublishing.com
www.moon-books.net

For distributor details and how to order please visit the 'Ordering' section on our website.

Text copyright: Mélusine Draco 2019

ISBN: 978 1 78904 407 2
978 1 78904 408 9 (ebook)
Library of Congress Control Number: 2019946981

A CIP catalogue record for this book is available from the British Library.

Design: Stuart Davies

UK: Printed and bound by CPI Group (UK) Ltd, Croydon, CR0 4YY
US: Printed and bound by Thomson-Shore, 7300 West Joy Road, Dexter, MI 48130

We operate a distinctive and ethical publishing philosophy in
all areas of our business, from our global network of authors to
production and worldwide distribution.

Contents

'There is an art of moving in the landscape, a right way to move around in it and approach places and monuments. Part of the sense of place is the action of approaching it from the 'right' direction.' The method of approach is governed by a combination of place and time – both seasonal and social – while the 'art' is the simultaneous practice of meditation and ritualized operation. 'Flashes of memory, so to speak, illuminate the occasion and bestows an instinctive grasp of how to behave within a ritual or sacred landscape, and to recognize the type of magical energy to be encountered there.' [*A Phenomenology of Landscape*, Christopher Tilley]

Mountains form the most spectacular creations on the planet and cover such a large amount of Earth's landmass that they can be seen clearly from outer space. Mountains are also a reminder that humans count for nothing in the greater scheme of things. They were formed by tectonic plate upheavals of such magnitude that the fossilised remains of prehistoric sea-creatures can be found on mountains tops; in fact, many Himalayan rocks were originally sediments on the primordial Tethys Ocean floor. In this first of the **Sacred Landscape** series we look at ways of connecting with the *genii locorum* that inhabit the caves and mountains of our world.

A companion volume to
Sacred Landscape: Groves & Forests **and** *Sacred Landscape: Lakes & Waterfalls.*

In memory of Noely ...
a creature of light and dark and shadow.

Prologue

I would never have the courage to be a mountaineer. And yet I am drawn to the sheer beauty and magnificence of mountains. They are the first things I see when I awake and the last things I see before I go to sleep, the shape of the range often silhouetted against the night sky, regardless of season. The view of them is never the same two days running and at certain times of the afternoon, the slopes are bathed in a strange, ethereal light that is nothing short of enchanting; the summits are either capped with snow; radiating the mellow tones of sunset; or shimmering in a soft blue haze, or cloaked by low-lying clouds and soft rain. On rare occasions, there are crystal clear images of a hot summer day when sheep are seen as tiny pin-pricks of white on the far-off slopes and patches of purple heather glow brightly in the sunshine.

The Galtee mountains of Ireland lack the rugged grandeur of the Prescellis, or the formidable bulk of the Black Mountain of Wales but as Aleister Crowley wrote:

'A mountain skyline is nearly always noble and beautiful, being the result of natural forces acting uniformly and in conformity with law ... A high degree of spiritual development, a romantic temperament and a profound knowledge based on experience of mountain conditions are the best safeguards against the insane impulses and hysterical errors which overwhelm the average man.'

Crowley developed his own love of mountains while a schoolboy scrambling among the rugged peaks of Wales, Scotland and the Lake District. He recorded in *Confessions*:

'My happiest moments were when I was alone on the

1

mountains; but there is no evidence that this pleasure in anyway derived from mysticism. The beauty of form and colour, the physical exhilaration of exercise, and the mental stimulation of finding one's way in difficult country, formed the sole elements of my rapture...'

Of the climb on the lower reaches of Chogo Ri [or K2] the second highest mountain in the world, after Mount Everest, he commented:

'The views are increasingly superb and the solitude was producing its beneficent results. The utterly disproportionate miniature of man purges him of smug belief in himself as the final cause of nature. The effect is it produces not humiliation but humility...'

Mountain worship is still central to certain indigenous religions in the world and the subject of many legends. For many, the most symbolic aspect of a mountain is the peak because it is believed that it is closest to heaven or other mystical worlds; while adverse weather conditions can give the slopes an almost forbidding attitude. Many beliefs are centred on sacred mountains, which either are, or were, considered holy (such as Mount Olympus in Greek mythology and Japan's Mount Fuji) or are related to famous events (like Mount Sinai in the Abrahamic religions). In some cases, the sacred mountain is purely mythical, like the Hara Berezaiti in Zoroastrianism, or Mount Kailash as the abode of the Hindu deity Shiva. Likewise, volcanoes, such as Mount Etna in Italy, were also considered sacred and believed to have been the home of Vulcan, the Roman god of fire and the forge.

Various cultures around the world maintain the importance of mountain worship and their sacredness - often in a complex system of mountain and ancestor worship - and a site of revelation and inspiration. Mountains are often viewed as the source of a power which is to be awed and revered. And perhaps we should all take the time to reflect on the words of Psalm 121:1 from the Old Testament in the King James Bible:

'I will lift up mine eyes unto the hills, from whence cometh my help...'

Mélusine Draco
Glen of Aherlow, 2018

Chapter One

First there is a mountain ...

In *A Phenomenology of Landscape* anthropologist Christopher Tilley describes the landscape as having ancestral importance due to it being such an integral part of human development that it abounds with cultural meaning and symbolism.

> 'Precisely because locales and their landscapes are drawn on in the day-to-day lives and encounters of individuals they possess powers. The spirit of place may be held to reside in a landscape.'

Despite different locations giving a variety of explanations for the existence of this 'spirit energy', in a large number of instances the intelligent, magical entity simply develops from the colloquially named 'spirit of place' over a great deal of time. He also observed:

> 'There is an art of moving in the landscape, a right way (socially constrained) to move around in it and approach places and monuments. Part of the sense of place is the action of approaching it from the 'right' (socially prescribed) direction.'

The method of approach is governed by a combination of place and time – both seasonal and social – while the 'art' is the simultaneous practice of meditation and ritualized operation. 'Flashes of memory', so to speak, illuminate the occasion and bestows an instinctive grasp of how to behave within a ritual or sacred landscape, and to recognize the type of magical energy to be encountered there.

Mountains form the most spectacular creations on the planet and cover such a large amount of Earth's landmass that they can be seen clearly from outer space. Mountains are also a reminder that humans count for nothing in the greater scheme of things. They were formed by tectonic plate upheavals of such magnitude that the fossilised remains of prehistoric sea-creatures can be found on the peaks; in fact, many Himalayan rocks were originally sediments on the primordial Tethys Ocean floor. And more recently, in 1980, a violent eruption tore apart the snow-capped peak of Mount St Helens in the USA, reminding us of the powerful, and often devastating, internal workings of this planet.

'Nevertheless, these spectacular rocky elevations have an enduring fascination and until relatively recently in man's evolution, people saw mountains and volcanoes as the homes of wrathful gods, who vent their anger without warning, shaking the ground, and spewing fire, rocks and ash into the air. Today, science tells us otherwise but our fascination with them continues, and they remain impressive and reminders of the spectacular power of Earth's continuing evolution.' [*Earth*, James F Luhr]

Two hundred million years ago all of the present continents were joined in a single landmass which geologists call Pangaea ('All-earth'). To the east, a great wedge-shape of the universal ocean cut deeply into this supercontinent; this vanished body of water takes its name from Tethys, the wife of Oceanus and the mother of the seas. Around 140 million years ago Pangaea began to break up and what we now recognise as the continents moved apart as a result of what science labelled 'continental drift'. It wasn't until 1968, as Chet Raymo explained in *The Crust of Our Earth*, that the old ideas of continental drift 'had found a secure place in the new and comprehensive theory of plate tectonics'.

As these landmasses slowly swirled around and bashed into one another at a rate of one or two inches per year, the force of this convergence crumpled continents and great mountain ranges, such as the Alps, Andes and Himalayas were pushed up. And explains why Darwin found fossil seashells embedded in sedimentary rock formations that could only have been laid down on the floor of an ancient sea at an elevation of 12,000 feet in the Andes.

The Himalaya, which contains the highest mountains on earth, had also long puzzled geologists as to the kind of force that could have so dramatically crumpled up this broad region of the earth's surface. The answer finally emerged from the theory of plate tectonics ... beginning about 40 million years ago and continuing today, the sub-continent of India has been involved in a colossal collision with the underside of Asia, throwing the margins of both landmasses high into the air! Since that time the growth of the Himalaya has continued to outpace erosion but eventually erosion *will* outpace the uplift and this magnificent mountain range will be cut down to size like the Appalachians, the Urals and other old ranges that mark the lines of earlier continental collisions.

Mankind has always been drawn to mountains as a sacred feature of the landscape. It's likely that mountains were among the oldest places of worship on the planet. They figure prominently in the earliest religious myths of mankind, and our connection to them is so powerful that many of the world's oldest folklore harks back to the mystique of the mountains. And yet for all their sacredness, mountains possess many natural forces with which to repel those who venture on to those hallowed slopes. Mountains can be inhospitable and dangerous places for the ill prepared. From one hour to the next, from one peak to the next, they can exhibit a dramatic variation in weather conditions from icy winds, low cloud and thick fog.

Mountains can deafen with an eerie silence and overwhelm

with their emptiness; distort time and space so that those climbing the slopes can lose all sense of where they are. These rocky peaks can bestow panoramas of breath-taking beauty, only to snatch them away again with an impassable rock face blocking the way. They cast dangerous rivers of scree; small rocks only held in place by light contact with neighbouring rocks that easily sweep the unwary away. Of all the weapons in the mountains' deadly armoury, none is more powerful, more absolute in its destruction than the divine retribution on those who venture too near the summit: mountain sickness

Is it not surprising then, that the mystique of the mountains is deeply ingrained in our psyche, despite the dangers associated with them? Trawling the internet, we find that several mountains are included on the 'most dangerous' listings. The International Mountaineering and Climbing Federation recognise 'eight-thousanders' as the fourteen mountains that are more than 8,000 metres (26,247 ft) in height above sea level in the 'death zone'; referring to altitudes above a certain point where the amount of oxygen is insufficient to sustain human life for an extended time span. All fourteen summits in the death zone are located in the Himalaya and Karakoram mountain ranges, where the most beautiful but deadly mountain-scapes include:

1. **Annapurna**'s avalanche-prone peak is the tenth highest in the world and the most statistically dangerous of its 8,000 meter companions. Annapurna is the goddess of food and nourishment in Hinduism Mount Annapurna in the Himalaya is named after this deadly daughter of Himavat, the king of the mountains

2. **K2** or **Chogori**, is the world's second highest mountain and known among climbers as one of the most technically difficult in the world. Ascents of even the easiest route require crossing a complicated glacier, ascending steep sections of rock, and negotiating a path

around a series of ice pillars which are prone to collapse without warning, makes it one of the most dangerous in the world. The remote K2 is known for bad weather and avalanches, claiming the lives of nearly 10% of those who attempt the ascent and when mountaineers talk of the deadly, difficult and hardest to climb mountains anywhere in the world, K2 tops the list. Considered to be the most beautiful for its massive pyramid like shape, local people view the Himalaya as both the embodiment and the realm of the gods and feel that disrespect for their sacred mountains has led to bad karma, restless spirits and a high death toll.

3. **Nanga Parbat** competes with K2 in terms of earning the mountain the nickname 'The Man Eater'. Also known affectionately as Killer Mountain, this craggy monster in Pakistan is an enormous ridge of rock and ice. Nanga Parbat is the ninth highest in the world, and its southern side is what many call the tallest mountain face on the planet. The mountain is a backdrop for the Fairy Meadows, where the legends of Nanga Parbat are kept alive, told by generations of villagers who have witnessed the legions of climbers who never descended its icy walls. 'When the sun shines, it smokes up there. The demons blow their horns and fairies cook their bread' says a local legend.

4. **Kangchenjunga**'s dramatic ridges, avalanches and bitter cold have made this one of the deadliest of mountains. Kangchenjunga is the third-tallest mountain in the world, with more than 200 summits and a 20% fatality rate. The fatality rates on the world's most dangerous mountains, tend to decrease as time goes on but one notable exception is Kangchenjunga, where death rates have reached as high as 22% in recent years, a reflection on the avalanche and weather hazards that plague its slopes. Besides being home to the iconic Kanchenjunga,

the State of Sikkim is rich with folklores and legends with one of the most famous being that of the *Yeti* or *Bon Manchi* that has confounded scientists and been a subject of fascination among travellers. According to legend, *Bon Manchi* is a 4-5 feet tall hairy creature who walks on two legs and can vanish into thin air. Locals are ardent believers of his existence and say that they have even heard his loud whistles. Lepchas, the original inhabitants of Sikkim revere the mountain, believing that they were all created by Kanchenjunga and there is a hidden paradise in the foothills where a Lepcha must return to after their earthly life is over.

5. **The Nordwand, or north face, of the Eiger** (which translates as 'Ogre') in the Swiss Alps is also legendary among mountaineers for its dangers. Though it was first climbed in 1938, the north face continues to challenge climbers of all abilities with both its technical difficulties and the heavy rockfalls that rake the face. The difficulty and hazards have earned the Eiger's north face the nickname Mordwand, or Murder Wall.

6. **The principal danger on the Matterhorn** is its popularity, with overeager tourists sending loose rocks onto the heads of fellow climbers below. Storms are also common during the afternoons and this mountain sees an average of about twelve deaths per year, with more than 500 since the first ascent. This iconic mountain, which looks like a horn rising out of the surrounding valleys, has one of the highest fatality rates of any peak in the Alps.

7. **Baintha Brakk** in Pakistan is considered another difficult mountain to climb and more than twenty failed attempts on the peak have earned it a reputation as being among the most dangerous in the world. It is like a giant tower, making it one of the steepest and the craggiest mountains to climb. Only three expeditions have

successfully summited Baintha Brakk because its steep walls and obstacles, combined with high altitude make it a hard nut to crack, hence the nickname 'the Ogre'.

8. **It would be easy to assume that Mount Everest** is the deadliest mountain of them all but the world's highest mountain claims a fairly small percentage of climbers considering the number of attempts every year. This congestion, when combined with Everest's extreme altitude, still makes it an undeniably dangerous objective.

9. **Denali** or **Mount. McKinley**, is the highest mountain in North America, also one of the most isolated and prominent in the world - and prone to earthquakes Though its altitude is only 20,320 feet, its high latitude means that the atmosphere is far thinner than it would be at the equator. For the many people who climb Denali each year, the altitude, weather, and extreme temperature pose a serious danger. For these reasons, the success rate on Denali is around 50% and more than 100 climbers have died attempting the summit. Humans have been living in Denali National Park for more than 11,000 years but the harsh winters mean that only a few archaeological sites have been preserved, but we know that the story of Denali's human inhabitants is a long one. In the last 500 years, the park was inhabited primarily by the Koyukon, Tanana and Dena'ina people who all called Denali mountain by a different word in their own languages. It was the Koyukon Athabaskans who referred to the huge, towering mountain as Dinale, which means 'tall one'.

10. **Cerro Chalten**, or **Mount FitzRoy**, is the tallest mountain in Patagonia's *Los Glaciares* National Park with its summit guarded on all sides by steep rock faces. For decades it was considered one of the most difficult mountains in the world and even today, the region's unpredictable weather and relative isolation makes it extremely dangerous.

As a result, FitzRoy may see only a single ascent in a year: truly the mark of a dangerous mountain. *Cerro* is a Spanish word meaning hill, while *Chaltén* comes from a Tehuelche word meaning 'smoking mountain', due to a cloud that usually forms around the peak.

11. **Siula Grande** is an imposing mountain in the Andes, with sheer south and west faces; the west face had seen several failed expeditions and was considered one of the most difficult climbs in South America. According to the records, the glaciers between Siula Grande and Yerupaja show a broad increase in the number, size and frequency of crevasses, and as a result, climbing routes used in the 1970s are today considered impracticable.

12. **Mount Washington** – called **Agiocochook** by some Native American tribes, is the highest peak in the north-eastern United States and the most deadly. Rapidly shifting weather, hurricane force winds, and summer ice pellets scouring the slopes have claimed more than 100 lives. Temperatures at the peak can descend to -50 degrees Fahrenheit: in fact, the strongest wind ever measured on Earth was recorded on this peak, a gale of 231 mph! The Abenaki people inhabiting the region at the time of the first European contact believed that the tops of mountains were the dwelling place of their gods, and did not climb them out of religious deference to their sanctity.

13. **Mont Blanc,** the tallest mountain in the Alps has a long history of climbing and climbing accidents. Mont Blanc is among the most heavily trafficked mountains in the world, with about 20,000 people summiting yearly but all of its routes have the hazards of falling rock and avalanches. During peak season, rescue services have been known to average twelve missions per weekend

and it has the highest fatality rate of any mountain in Europe, with estimates at 100 deaths per year. It's been said that the reason for the mountain's deadliness is the frequent portrayal of it as a 'long walk' and not a challenging climb.

This is the dark and deadly nature of mountains – lofty, majestic and unforgiving. And although there is often little recorded myth and legend surrounding these 'monsters' people who live in their shadow usually consider them to be both protective and sacred. The summit of a mountain has long been viewed as the dwelling place of the gods and probably explains why few indigenous people ever ventured into this forbidding territory above the clouds, since adverse weather conditions on the higher slopes would also have made them almost impenetrable.

Nevertheless, there *is* something about mountains that makes them truly inspiring. imposing and remote, towering above the plains, they *are* majestic and awesome - and literally form a stairway to heaven - acting as the gateway to the heavens. Eternally exposed to the elements and the vagaries of the weather, yet ever enduring, mountains seem to teach us what equanimity in the face of adverse conditions is all about. Every climb up a mountain is an exercise in spiritual growth and as we leave behind the dross and the mundane to scale the peak in search of another dimension, the mountain doubles as a metaphor for life. The towering mountain peak may be in our sights at all times but it has to be climbed one step at a time with persistence, tenacity and a never-say-die spirit.

The Magic of Mountains in Art

Needless to say, mountains also inspire art in all its forms – and since the most important cult-centres of the Muses were on mountains or hills, we should still look towards these sacred landscapes for inspiration. There is a wealth of **literature** about or inspired by mountains and it's easy to see why. One only has to think of a mountain and the powerful adjectives tumble around in our imagination: solitary, ancient, vast, god-like, majestic … The 'literature of the Five Mountains' is that produced by the principal Zen monastic centres of the Rinzai sect in Kyoto and Kamakura, and is used collectively to refer to the poetry and prose produced by Japanese monks during the 14th and 15th centuries.

And just as rivers often represent the flow of life, so too the mountain is a handy metaphor - for the insignificance of man perhaps, or as a reminder that ours is a planet built on nature's awesome violence,' wrote Ben Myers in the *Guardian* …

'The role of mountains in literature is multifarious. They can be symbolic or metaphorical, or they can simply provide a dramatic setting. They can be friend, or, in the case of Sherlock Holmes who met his death at the Reichenbach Falls in the Swiss Alps, they can be killer. Consider the sense of imprisonment that the Carpathians created in Bram Stoker's *Dracula*, the escape route that the high plateau of Tibet provided in Heinrich Harrer's *Seven Years In Tibet*, or the place of solace offered by Wyoming's fictional *Brokeback Mountain* in Annie Proulx's short story of the same name.'

Ernest Hemingway opens his 1936 short story 'The Snows of Kilimanjaro' by mentioning a leopard carcass up near the summit of Mount Kilimanjaro in Africa:

'Close to the western summit there is the dried and frozen carcass of a leopard. No one has explained what the leopard was seeking at that altitude ...'

It has been suggested that the leopard was also symbolic of all that is strong, noble, and courageous; it dies in a symbolic quest to find the 'House of God' in the Masai language.

Ancient authors and modern writers, poets and playwrights invoke 'the Muse' when writing tragedy (Melpomene), comedy (Thalia) epic poetry (Calliope) and history (Clio). If evoking the Muses use either a large rock as an altar in a local grove or a classical statue on a pedestal in the garden.

For centuries, the grandeur of mountain scenery has mesmerised artists in search of images to convey the infinite in **paintings.** Mountains amaze and delight us, inspiring the human mind to peaks of excitement and curiosity. 'Apparently it took the Romantic movement to make mountains seem mysterious in their wildness, tempting in their danger' wrote Jonathan Jones, also for the *Guardian* ...

'This is one area of the imagination where artists seem to have been ahead of the crowd. Some of them were depicting and even exploring the marvellous mountains much earlier. Leonardo da Vinci climbed in the Alps and in his paintings mountains – glimpsed through a rocky cavern in the *Virgin of the Rocks* or revealed as a ravishing ethereal vista in the *Virgin and Child with St Anne* – are images of the psyche and the infinite. Another Renaissance artist who had a feel for mountains was Titian – in his paintings the blue shadows of Alpine foothills are seen with acute longing and love. Trees on a hilltop, against a blue sky, and a town overlooking a valley – details such as these make Titian a true lover of wild scenery.

Both these artists came from hill towns. But other artists too found mountains unforgettable. A lot of the time, in Renaissance art, a mountain is just a sharp jagged dry rock. Hermits live in savage mountain wastes. But there is also a sense of the hills as places of fantasy and the unknown. The romantic discovery of mountains was not as sudden as all that, at least in art. Surely there is no more magical celebration of mountains than Giambologna's statue that personifies the Apennines as a colossal bearded man, a giant whose face is darkly enigmatic. The original mountain man, it has wandered out of those distant yet magnetic, forbidding yet seductive Leonardoesque hills.'

And yet the painting of the Far East reflects the mystery of mountains from early times. *Shan shui*, literally meaning 'mountain-water' refers to a style of traditional Chinese painting that involves or depicts scenery or natural landscapes, using a brush and ink rather than more conventional paints. Mountains, rivers and often waterfalls are prominent in this art form. First developed in the 5th century, these landscape paintings usually centred on mountains that had long been seen as sacred places in China, being viewed as the homes of immortals and thus, close to the heavens.

Similarly, nature, and specifically mountains have also been a favourite subject of Japanese art since its earliest days and an image of a natural scene is not just a landscape, but rather a portrait of the sacred world, and the *kami* who live within it. Perhaps nothing is as spectacular as the perfect conical shape of the slumbering volcano, Mount Fuji, and the very real threat of its deadly fury, combining in an awe-inspiring entity that has been worshipped and painted for centuries, or the reoccurring theme of mist filling the middle ground, and in the background, mountains far in the distance. In *Spirituality of Mountain Art in Japan: Buddhism, Shintoism, and Contemplation*, Lee Jay Walker observes that in Japan:

'...the mountainside is a place where Buddhism and Shintoism can fuse with nature and provide solitude, escapism, religious reflections, provide an escape from the stresses of life, and other factors ...'

And yet perhaps the most captivating of all is the *Broken Ink Landscape* scroll - a painting on a hanging scroll made by the Japanese artist Sesshū Tōyō in 1495. The painter avoids strongly defined outlines, with shapes indicated by colour washes in lighter and darker tones as the work slowly reveals itself to the viewer.

'Emerging from the undefined forms is the suggestion of misty mountains in the background. In the foreground are cliffs and bushes, and the triangular roofline and sloping banner for a wine shop with vertical lines forming a fence. Beneath is the flat surface of a body of water, with two people in a rowing boat.'

And yet it seems strange to think that the Western appetite for these lofty heights is something invented by modern culture. We would think that the awe and grandeur of mountain scenery was a universal instinct, but art historians tell us that before the 18th century Europeans *dreaded* mountains. Until then they were seen 'as ugly raw wildernesses of stone, murderous enemies of cultivated life'.

There wasn't a specific classic god or goddess of the visual arts. Hephaestus was the god of artisans and sculptors, among other things; while the goddess Athena, represented creativity and the arts. A small libation can be offered on the altar stone or pedestal.

Music has also been inspired by mountains with dozens of classical pieces from symphonies to tone poems creating the ambiance and magic of mountainous landscapes. The stunning scenery, history and culture of Europe's lakes, mountains and rivers has inspired many musicians, nor to mention the millions of 20th-century listeners who owe their initial acquaintance with Mussorgsky's tone-poem to Leopold Stokowski's version, *Night on Bald Mountain*, specially produced for Walt Disney's 1940 film *Fantasia*. Or as Dick Sullivan wrote:

'Music can convey emotions better than poetry or prose and what I'm trying to convey is an emotion. To understand it better, therefore, perhaps you should stand on the Malvern Hills where Piers Plowman went one May morning ('in a summer season when soft was the sun') and look across the green counties while listening to Vaughan Williams's *The Lark Ascending* and *The Thomas Tallis Suite*. Then you can both see and feel what I'm trying so clumsily to say.' [*The Victorian Web*]

And perhaps we should think about how many popular songs with 'mountain' in the title have been written and listed by ranker.com including songs like *Wild Mountain Thyme* by Francis McPeake, *Rocky Mountain High* by John Denver and *Ain't No Mountain High Enough* by Marvin Gaye.

The Muses for music and song (Euterpe), hymns (Polyhymnia), and dance (Terpsicore) and a small libation can be offered on the altar stone or pedestal.

Similarly, the PoemHunter.com lists a hundred **poems** inspired by mountains … and how could there not be? The sublime majesty of mountains has inspired history's best minds, proving William Blake's dictum: 'Great things are done when men and mountains meet' and where the poets are 'metaphorical mountaineers, grappling with the inconceivable power of mountains, attempting to achieve the summit of understanding'.

Li Bai, the legendary Chinese poet, uses mountains to great effect in many of his poems. One of his most famous, titled variously as *Green Mountain* or *In the Mountains*, perfectly captures the serene solitude that people find on mountain tops. [*The Clymb*]

'You ask me why I dwell in the green mountain;
I smile and make no reply for my heart is free of care.
As the peach-blossom flows down stream and is gone into
the unknown,
I have a world apart that is not among men.'

This brief journey through the world's mountain-scapes reveals the extent of their influence, regardless of culture or creed, from the past, or in the present. Mountains are sacred, the spiritual home of deities, and/or the final resting place of our cultural ancestors. And there are those who would make the ultimate sacrifice by venturing too close to this habitat of the gods and perish in the attempt. Mountains have been the inspiration for painters, musicians, writers and poets and even if we do not have access to the magnificence of these edifying peaks, the magic of the art they create can put us in touch with the Divine.

The Muses invoked for love poetry (Erato), lyric poetry (Euterpe) a small libation can be also be offered on the altar stone or pedestal.

We can use these various art forms to help forge the right ambiance for creativity, or log on to YouTube https://www.youtube.com/watch?v=2R2gb0MKJlo&feature=share for *10 Hours Of Relaxing Planet Earth II Mountain Sounds | Earth Unplugged*bc to create the perfect visualisation to the actual voice of the mountains without human or musical soundtrack.

Mystical Interlude: Earth Mysteries

What exactly do we mean by Earth Mysteries? Is it an overwhelming love of the planet which has spawned charities, political parties, numerous magazines and countless green-eco groups? Is it part of the 1990s mega-myth that the Earth cannot fend for herself and that if world governments do not take heed of pollution and global warming, then Gaia is heading for destruction? Is it really taking part in an 'Earth Healing Day' by sitting in a meditative trance to channel combined energies into closing the wounds made through greed and commercial exploitation? Or is it a pilgrimage to a sacred site to plug into the power emanating from the Ancestors?

In 'The Pathway of Nuit' published in *Phoenix* Magazine, Dr. Mériém Clay-Egerton took a far more brutal and far-reaching view of humanity and its puny efforts to survive.

'The planet is shaking itself free, initially to try and eradicate the parasites which are disturbing it … All that *homo sapiens* have produced now bucks, wavers and breaks down, and will finally disappear. It is no longer a bright and proud future, but dark and sullen. The Earth realises that to free herself she must first destroy herself and start again with new building bricks. But she can't tell the guilty from the innocent, so all will go as they must into infinity…'

But to return to the popular concept of Earth Mysteries … and before conjuring up the inevitable picture of some weird figure doing something 'strange in the woods', perhaps it is easier to refer to Shinto, the indigenous religion of Japan for a universally accepted and comparable example of a 'living' nature belief. Essentially a compound of ancestor and nature worship, Shinto's silent contemplation of a flower, stream, rock formation or sunset is, in itself, a normal, everyday act of private worship. As part of a national ritual, each year at the blossoming of the cherry trees, thousands of Japanese leave the city to enjoy the beauty of the short-lived flowering. Neither is it uncommon for them to spend a whole evening gazing at the moon; or sit for hours 'listening to the stones grow'. Inconsiderately, some might think, Shinto shrines are usually to be found in remote locations of breathtaking natural beauty – with little thought for the convenience of the worshipper.

For the traditional Japanese there is no dividing line between the divine and human, since the forces that move in Nature, move in man according to Zen teaching:

'When one looks at it, one cannot see it:
When one listens for it, one cannot hear it:
However, when one uses it, it is inexhaustible.'

Even rocks are possessed of the divine spark and often form part of the intricate designs used to create those familiar Zen temple gardens for contemplation – reflecting the belief that the Buddha-nature is immanent not only in man, but in everything that exists, animate or inanimate.

Recognizing this instinctive feel for the divine spark of spirituality inherent in Nature is one of the fundamental abilities of those with a pagan mind set. A solitary walk by a rushing spring stream; the awesome thrill of an approaching thunderstorm in late summer; a stroll through the woods in autumn; or the first snow fall on the mountains are times for the working of natural magic. Nevertheless, these natural phenomena can make even the most blasé of people hanker for more of these feelings of elation that can grow from the experience of coming into contact with Earth Mysteries.

When referring to Earth Mysteries, it is also necessary to understand the difference between a 'place of power', and a sacred or historical site. For example, a large number of modern pagans treat any ancient earthworks as such, without any prior knowledge of its religious antecedents. As a traditional witch of my acquaintance once pointed out to her flock, such activities are on a par with worshipping at a castle moat or Neolithic flint quarry! Simply because something is old does not mean it has, or had, any religious or spiritual significance.

And as Philip Heselton explained in *The Elements of Earth Mysteries*, this is a living subject.

'It is not just a study of things in the past, but is something now, in the present, and moreover something that involves our own participation: we 'become' involved. The visiting of sites and our interaction with the landscape comes central to our belief. What we are dealing with is a recognition that there are special places in the landscape that are in some way qualitatively special. Whilst we may not be able to define this exactly, we know when we visit them that this is true. Whether we can detect the energies present at such a site depends on many factors, particularly the cyclical nature of such energies in the landscape and in ourselves'.

'One of the insights provided by Earth Mysteries is the finding of significance in one's 'local' landscape, to find contentment and happiness at one's local sacred sites and, for that moment,, to put aside all desire to be elsewhere, be it Stonehenge, Glastonbury, or wherever, and to know the truth that you are the centre of the universe and that wherever you are, is where you should be.' [*What You Call Time*]

Another easy way to 'plug-in' to these earth energies is to bond with something that reaches deep down into the ground, a standing stone or a very old tree, for example. It's rather alarming the first time it happens because it's usually an unintentional, unexpected and highly physical experienced. Squatting down and leaning back against the tree or rock we become aware of

21

this terrifically strong pulse-beat and the immediate reaction s to move because we think we are inadvertently pressing on a nerve. We shift our position and the pulse-beat is still there; we re-arrange ourselves but the beat goes on, as they say in the words of the jazz-men.

Having recognised that this *is* an 'outside' sensation, we should be able to feel the pulsation with our hands, just as if we were placing the palms of our hand against the rib cage of an extremely large animal. It's a simple method of coming to terms with the fact that the trees and rocks are 'alive' with an inner core of vibrant energy.

Chapter Two

Where the Light Has Never Shone

Caves play an important role in the story of humanity. In addition to providing shelter for our earliest ancestors, caves were often considered to be an entrance to mystical realms. For some cultures, caves were the gateways to the underworld, while others believed that supernatural beings dwelled within. Nevertheless, there are numerous craggy outcroppings and ranges of hills that add beauty and majesty to a landscape – and beneath them often lie miles of secret caves carved out of natural rock by primordial waters.

The tectonic forces that lead to mountain building are continuously countered by erosion due to intensified precipitation, wind and temperature extremes. These elements, aided by the force of gravity, are particularly powerful along mountain ranges; rainwater also mixes with chemicals as it falls from the sky, forming an acidic concoction that dissolves rock. For example, acid rain dissolves limestone to form karst, a type of terrain filled with fissures, underground streams and caves – and once such a cave is formed, stalactites and stalagmites may begin to form. Exploring deep caves is a wonderful way of connecting with our ancient, natural world – even those that were man-made. For example:

Devetashka Cave in Bulgaria has provided shelter for groups of humans since the late Paleolithic era, and continuously for tens of thousands of years since then; the earliest traces of human presence date back to the middle of the Early Stone Age around 70,000 years ago.

Beautiful stalactites and stalagmites, rivulets, majestic natural domes and arches can be found within the enormous cave making it understandable why various human populations would have chosen Devetashka as their home.

By comparison, **Uplistsikhe**, whose name translates to 'Fortress of the Lord', was an ancient rock-hewn town which played a significant role in Georgian history over a period of some 3,000 years. Beginning its history in the 2nd millennium, Uplistsikhe has been identified as one of the oldest urban settlements in Georgia when the complex was a very important cultural centre for pagan worship in Iberia. Archaeologists have unearthed numerous temples and findings relating to a sun goddess, worshipped prior to the arrival of Christianity. The ancient cave city was built on a rocky bank of the Mtkvari River where the rock-cut structures include dwellings, a large hall and functional buildings, such as a bakery, a prison, cellars, and even an amphitheatre, all connected by footways and tunnels. Between the 6th century BCE and 11th century CE, Uplistsikhe was one of the most important political, religious, and cultural centres of pre-Christian Kartli and flourished until it was ravaged by the Mongols in the 13th century.

Some of the planet's most wonderful natural cave-systems range from the **Hang Son Doong** cave in Vietnam that is so big it has its own river, jungle and climate - to the magical **Fingal's Cave** located on Staffa in Scotland that is famous for its distinctive hexagonal basalt columns; the sea-cave's size, shape, and naturally-arched roof combine with the waves to create eerie sounds that enhance its cathedral-like atmosphere.

Others are known for strange phenomena like the **Blue Grotto** on Capri, unique for its brilliant blue glow which comes from two sources: the entrance to the cave (a small opening where only one rowboat can enter at a time) and a bigger hole beneath the entrance. When viewed from inside the cave, the entrance appears as a brilliant white light just above the waterline, while the underwater hole, which is the larger source of light, provides a blue glow.

Or the fascinating **Cave of the Crystals** in Chihuahua, Mexico, containing the largest natural selenite crystals ever found - the biggest being twelve meters in length and four meters in diameter! Thanks to the pool of magma beneath the cave, the groundwater remained at 50 degrees Celsius for 500,000 years, allowing selenite crystals to form and grow to gigantic sizes. The cave was only ever accessible because of the pumping operations of a local mining company and now that mining had ceased, the cave has since been re-flooded in an attempt to return it to an undisturbed state in which its crystals can continue to grow.

Eisriesenwelt Ice Cave in Austria is a natural limestone ice cave and the largest of its kind, extending forty-two kilometers into the earth. Although the cave is massive, only the first kilometer of it is covered in ice and open to tourists. The rest of the cave is just limestone but the oldest layer of ice dates back 1,000 years! Eisriesenwelt was formed by the Salzach river, which slowly eroded passageways in the mountain; the ice formations in the cave were created by thawing snow that drained into the cave and froze. This section remains icy even in the summer because the cave entrance is open year-round, leaving it exposed to chilly winds that keep the temperature below freezing. New formations appear each spring, however, as water drips into the cave and freezes.

The **Puerto Princesa Subterranean River** in the Philippines is one of the New Seven Wonders of Nature and a UNESCO World Heritage Site. In 2010, a group of environmentalists and geologists discovered that the underground river has a second floor, creating numerous small waterfalls inside the cave. There is also a 300-meter cave dome above the underground river and unbelievable rock formations, a deep hole in the river, secondary river channels, and another deep cave. There are also several large chambers found inside the cave, including the 360-meter Italian Chamber, which is one of the most massive cave rooms in the world. The river in the cave is navigable by boat for up to four kilometers, but it is impossible to explore any further due to a critical lack of oxygen.

Mammoth Cave's discovery goes back 4000 years since the first humans to enter descended into its winding passages. On the surface, Mammoth National Park in central Kentucky encompasses around 80 square miles, but underneath lies a twisting labyrinth of limestone caves, creating a network that earns the title of the longest cave system in the world. 600km miles of the cave have been explored to date, but no one knows how far the cave system actually extends, as new caverns and recesses are continuously being discovered. One of the cave's most remarkable features is the abundance of stalactite formations, which number in the thousands and created from years of water seeping through the cave's limestone ceiling.

The **Krubera Cave** in Georgia was the deepest-known cave on the planet, with a depth of over 2196 meters. Krubera cave is also known as the Voronja Cave, which means 'cave of the crows' in Russian because of a number of crows nesting at the entrance of the cave. Since the discovery of **Veryovkina Cave** in the same area of Abkhazia that was discovered to have a depth of 2212 meters, this is now the deepest cave in the world.

Škocjan Cave is home to some of the most significant underground phenomena both in the Karst region and Slovenia, earning it a spot as a protected UNESCO World Heritage Site. International scientific circles consider it to be one of the most important natural treasures on the planet because it is among the largest underground canyons known worldwide as well as being historically and culturally significant because it was inhabited during prehistoric times.

Sistema Ox Bel Ha, Mexico is the largest under-water cave in the world and its walls are dark brown in color because of the 'tannic acid' in the water. Bordered by the Savannah wetlands and the mangrove swamps, the majority of the cave system is located deep under the jungle and although these passages are not been accessible, some are connected directly with the

Caribbean Sea.

And yet the strangest must surely be **Prohodna Cave** in Bulgaria. This cave is a popular tourist attraction due to a certain natural feature, i.e. two eye-shaped holes in its central chamber. These holes, which are almond-shaped and symmetrical, are reckoned to resemble the eyes of a human being and have been commonly referred to as the 'Eyes of God'. On a clear night the moon can be seen through the eyes, which can be a scary and overwhelming experience.

So ... which is the largest cave in the world? **Sarawak Chamber** was until after extensive laser scanning, cave explorers had a different cave to nominate: the **Miao Room Cavern**, a chamber beneath China's Ziyun Getu He Chuandong National Park, accessible only by an underground stream. Nevertheless, the **Mulu Caves**, located in Gunung Mulu National Park on the island of Borneo, are home to the world's largest cave chamber by *surface* area, as well as one of the largest cave passages on earth. The Sarawak Chamber, which is so large that it could hold 40 Boeing 747 airplanes; or the **Deer Chamber**, one of the largest cave passages so big it could fit five cathedrals the size of Saint Paul's in London inside its cavernous walls.

Although the most impressive of all those mentioned must surely be **Son Doong Cave** - one of the largest caves, measuring over 5.5 miles in length with some of its caverns large enough to hold a 40-story skyscraper. The cave is also home to a virgin jungle growing more than 600 feet beneath the Earth's surface, in a portion of the cave where the roof has collapsed, allowing natural sunlight to filter down. Plants both small and large can thrive in the cave jungle - with trees growing nearly 100 feet tall. A river flowing inside gives this wonder its name in English, meaning 'Mountain River Cave'.

No doubt there are many other caves – large and small, man-made and natural - around the world that have their own mystical character that remain tantalisingly beyond our understanding. One such place is the prehistoric underground Hypogeum on Malta where Frater M was able to strip away all previous archaeological theories and reveal (to himself) the true secrets of this mysterious place and recorded in *What You Call Time*.

> 'The Hypogeum is bursting with unexplained, enigmatic mysteries. The deepest part of the site is forty feet below ground reached via a series of steps, narrow ledges and deep pits. The innermost chamber is a high vaulted room about nine feet in diameter and cut into the walls at floor level are five small arch-like openings just large enough to admit an adult, which leads into circular pits about three feet deep that archaeologists have described as burial pits or storage for grain.'

During his first visit, Frater M found himself alone in what was termed 'The Oracle room' by the guidebooks, standing by an arch-shaped hollow at face level – approximately fourteen-inches across x eighteen-inches high and twelve-inches in depth; the hollow had a curved top but straight bottom. He discovered that when a man speaks into this chamber a resonance is set up that reverberates – not only in the Oracle Room but throughout the Temple. If a woman speaks into the chamber, nothing occurs.

> 'Archaeologists (working on the principle that the priests of old were charlatans leading a cretinous mass) say that this accidental or lucky design was used to frighten the congregation into subservience and belief of the oracle's power. The reverberation produced is certainly impressive and would put to shame an electric synthesizer, so great is its power. Being an occultist and sensitive to ethereal vibrations, it soon became obvious that a mystical happening was about to occur.

I was standing alone in the Oracle Room trying to appreciate how these so-called 'primitives' could have known how to obtain such a fantastic sonic effect when I began to receive information that brought insight from the inner planes. Moving to the lip of rock opposite the reverberation chamber, I pressed my shoulder against the end of it and could see straight into the chamber. *This was how the Oracle worked* – there was no need to stick your head into the chamber; it was more perfect than the archaeologists knew.'

Humming in a deep voice, Frater M directed it across the room into the reverberation chamber and the reverberations picked up instantly; this time much louder than the effect of speaking directly into the chamber. There was more to discover – there was an oscillation there and humming again for a longer period, the oscillation built up into a rhythm.

'My head began to buzz and in an instant, I knew what I had to do. This overlooked Oracle Room was a mantra resonator which had been specifically designed to effectively and speedily jack-up the High Priest's consciousness (and that of others in the rest of the Temple in a secondary way). Anybody in the Oracle Room would have been 'gone' in several minutes. The congregation probably stood in the main chamber and got the side effects.

Then it hit me. The High Priest wouldn't just mumble any old rubbish: it would be the basic phonetic mantra of the Cult. It would be *ma* and I began to reiterate this most fundamental of sound-concept ideas and the room came alive. Within a couple of minutes, I was in a semi-trance state and in a flash she was there. Over in the first chamber the High Priestess, curled up in an embryonic pose. From my position, without altering my gaze or mantra, I could see right into the chamber that was the obvious Womb of the Mother Goddess. For a split second *She* was there!

It was perfect: the reverberation could only work with a masculine voice. The priest organised the thing but the priestess was the only one who could divine the Will of the Goddess and reach full possession state. Via the masculinity of the priest's voice, the potency of the sound activated the trance state of the priestess and she received the guidance of the gods. It was sacred.' [*The Great Goddess Rediscovered*]

Without his extensive occult training Frater M would probably not have been able to 'tune in' to the psychic vibrations emanating from the underground chamber; an inexperienced person making the same discovery by accident would more than likely have been terrified out of their wits. And despite his vast experience of psychic phenomena, however, it still took about four hours for Frater M to totally regain his equilibrium.

There is a marked different, however, between a sacred (temple) site and an ancient (burial) monument. Sacred sites become sacred by a dedicated usage, while other places may have been consecrated for a specific use. The building of megalithic monuments such as Maes Howe (Orkney) and New Grange (Ireland) burial sites are prime examples. Rituals held in the past would have been purely dedicated to the cult of the ancestors and the deities deemed to have been concerned with death and possibly rebirth. It seems unlikely that such funerary sites would have been visited for anything other than the rites for which they were designed.

At the other end of the sacred/ancestral spectrum to the Maltese temple is Paviland cave on the Gower peninsula in South Wales, and a crucial site for tracing the origins of human life in Britain. It was in here, in 1823, that William Buckland, the first Professor of Geology at Oxford University, excavated the remains of a body that had been smeared with red ochre (naturally occurring iron oxide) and buried with a selection of periwinkle shells and ivory rods. The headless skeleton was given the name – 'the Red Lady of Paviland' – and it is still called the Red Lady, even though we now know two things Buckland didn't: the remains are those of a young *man*, probably in his late 20s, and they were buried 34,000 years ago, making the 'Red Lad' the oldest anatomically modern human skeleton found in Britain, and marking Paviland as the site of the oldest ceremonial burial in western Europe.

Excavators who came after Buckland also found over 4000 worked flints, necklace bones, stone needles and mammoth-ivory bracelets on the floor of the cave, suggesting it was in regular use, even though a few thousand years after the Red Lad was buried temperatures fell further. The ice advanced and Britain was abandoned by early man, leaving the cave's occupant to lie alone for thousands of years. The ivory rods clearly had some ritualistic or artistic use since they weren't hunting tools or weapons, which led to the belief that his role was of either religious significance or as a leader of some sort ... that he was a mammoth hunter, who got killed and was buried by his companions. Nevertheless, this prehistoric burial site deserves our respect for the importance of its occupant.

Of much more recent creation, Royston Cave is a small artificial chamber in Hertfordshire, although it is not known who created it or what it was used for. First discovered in August 1742 when a worker was digging footings for a new bench at a butter market, he uncovered a millstone and when he dug around to remove it, he found the shaft leading to the cave. It was half-filled with dirt and rock but once the rubble was removed, workers discovered numerous sculptures and carvings, dating back as early as 1200 CE. The images are mostly religious, depicting St. Catherine, the Holy Family, the Crucifixion, St. Lawrence holding the gridiron on which he was martyred, and a figure holding a sword who could be either St. George or St. Michael.

Elsewhere in the tiny cave are other, non-Christian carvings including the figures of a horse and a rather risqué *Sheela-na-gig*, an ancient pagan fertility symbol. The most popular theory, however, is that the chamber was carved and used by the Knights Templar; a large panel is believed to be a memorial to the last Grand Master, Jacques de Molay, who was burned for heresy in 1314 in Paris. The Templars were certainly prominent in the area, having strongholds nearby and there are many Templar-inspired images on the cave walls.

The on-going mystery of what is represented inside the cave is equalled by the mystery of what was once situated *above* it. Royston Cave is located below the crossing of two ancient roads: Ermine Street, the Old North Road, which ran from London to Lincoln and on to York; and the Icknield Way, a prehistoric trackway following the chalk escarpment, believed to be the oldest road in Britain. While *Axis of Heaven* points out that Royston is strategically located on the St Michael Line (an alignment of numerous ancient sites) and the Greenwich Meridian (or the old Axis Mundi of England).

Despite its flaws, however, most serious researchers lean towards the theory that Royston Cave was a Knights Templar chapel, perhaps even a replica of the Holy Sepulchre Church in Jerusalem, complete with an altar in the west and an assortment of cult figures decorated by none other than the Templar themselves. Supporters of the theory cite the fact that the Templars were in Royston most weeks, from at least 1199 onwards, and maintained churches in neighbouring villages. Adding credence to this theory is the fact that the Templars were in conflict with the Priory of Royston, whose clergy were known to have later imprisoned Knights from nearby Baldock. The Knights Templar would have needed a private place to meet on market days and the cave beneath the market cross would, in many ways, have been the perfect spot.

Equally mysterious are the markings discovered recently by cavers when the group visited

Creswell Crags (a limestone gorge on the Nottinghamshire/ Derbyshire border) with other underground enthusiasts from the group Subterranea Britannica. In Robin Hood Cave, amidst the profusion of historic graffiti on the cave walls, they noticed some markings that reminded them of those found in caves under the Mendip Hills in Somerset. The markings include hundreds of letters, symbols and patterns carved at a time when belief in witchcraft was widespread; the scale and variety of the marks made on the limestone walls and ceiling of a cave which has at its centre a deep, dark hole, is unprecedented.

Commonly known as 'witch marks' these apotropaic scratchings (from the Greek *apotrepein* meaning 'to turn away'), are most commonly found carved on stone or woodwork near a building's doorways, windows and fireplaces, to protect inhabitants and visitors from evil spirits. A few have been recorded at Shakespeare's birthplace and spotted in medieval barns like those at Bradford-on-Avon Tithe Barn, where they were etched into the ancient timber to protect crops. Heritage experts believe them to be the biggest concentration of apotropaic marks, or symbols to ward off evil or misfortune, ever found in the UK.

Duncan Wilson, Chief Executive of Historic England said of the discovery:

'Creswell Crags is already of international importance for its Ice Age art and ancient remains. To find this huge number of protection marks from the more recent past adds a whole new layer of discovery. Even two hundred years ago the English countryside was a very different place, death and disease were everyday companions and evil forces could readily be imagined in the dark. One can only speculate on what it was that the people of Creswell feared might emerge from the underworld into these caves.'

The engravings and paintings represent the first known flowering of cave art. The spectacular limestone gorge is thought to have been occupied by as early as 43,000 BCE. This network of caves, weathered deep into the rock, no doubt provided shelter from the harsh conditions of the last Ice Age, and the area is now home to Britain's most important collection of occupation sites from this period. The first 'hint' of Creswell's ancient art was found in 1876, when Victorian antiquarians discovered what has become known as the Ochre Horse, an engraving on a rib bone hidden in the caves at Creswell. However, it was not until 2003 that Britain's only confirmed examples of Ice Age cave art were discovered

The Magical World of Cave Art

The first painted cave acknowledged as being Paleolithic, meaning from the Stone Age, was at Altamira in Spain, where the art discovered there was deemed by experts to be the work of modern humans (Homo sapiens). Most examples of cave art have been found in France and in Spain, but a few are also known in Portugal, England, Italy, Romania, Germany and Russia with the total number of known sites being about four-hundred.

Most cave art consists of paintings made with either red or black pigment. The reds were made with iron oxides (hematite), whereas manganese dioxide and charcoal were used for the blacks. Cave art is now generally considered to have a symbolic or ritual function, sometimes both. The exact meanings of the images remain unknown, but no doubt were created within the framework of shamanic beliefs and practices. One such practice involved going into a deep cave for a ceremony during which a shaman would enter a trance state and send his or her soul into the otherworld to make contact with the spirits and try to obtain their guidance.

Examples of paintings and engravings in deep caves - i.e. existing completely in the darkness -are rare outside Europe but are suggestive of being the forerunner of the chthonic beliefs of the Greeks and the deities of the Under/Otherworld. And as Professor H W Janson observes in *A History of Art*, hidden away as they are in the bowels of the earth, to protect them from the casual intruder, these images must have served a purpose far more serious than mere decoration.

'One of the most important and useful factors inherent in the study of rock or cave art is that its location has not changed – it is still where the artist chose to put it and the viewer is occupying the same space that the artist occupied. This can give us a great deal of information that is far more solid and dependable than speculations about meaning.

One must always bear in mind the role played in any culture by features of the landscape or of a site which were associated with particular myths or legends or events, traditional or tribal territories, sacred or holy areas or taboos. Similarly, in any culture there may be 'good' places and 'bad' places, and even inside caves there were probably places where such intangible factors played an important role in the decoration of the walls.

The natural architecture of caves played a role in the way in which they were decorated ... and the ultimate example of this phenomenon is evident in the Pergouset Cave where the engraved art begins only after a long crawl, at full stretch, down a narrow, low, wet and unpleasant passage. One of the engraved figures, a horse head, was made at arm's length inside a fissure into which the artist could not possibly have inserted their head. Even the artist never saw this figure: it was not meant to be seen by human eyes.' [*Art & Religion in the Stone Age*]

What archaeologist, Paul Bahn finds even more intriguing are the numerous images that were *purposely* hidden, up high chimneys, under low overhangs or in niches. 'Such imagery was not made to be seen by other Stone Age people, but was intended to be seen by – or was offered to – something else, perhaps a deity, spirit or ancestor. In other words, some cave art (but not necessarily all of it) was clearly religious in some way and produced out of strongly held motivations'. In fact, inaccessibility appears to be the crucial factor for this 'hidden' imagery. Perhaps the overcoming of obstacles, the discomforts and dangers, were more important than the actual creation of the images.

Perhaps, too, the placing of the images in the most inaccessible location possible was somehow linked to the remoteness of the artist's everyday world – and it was the remoteness that made the images as sacred as possible. There is even a suggestion that this exquisite cave art wasn't meant to last and that its survival was irrelevant. This could certainly be true of Le Tuc d'Audoubert where the now-famous clay bison were made at the far end of the cave, after an arduous journey of nine-hundred metres – the farthest point that could be reached. The images were left in the darkness, and it is doubtful whether anyone ever returned to see them until their discovery in the early 20th century.

And we should take Frater M's experience in the Hypogeum in Malta into account when we study Bahn's comments about another factor which may have played a significant role in the choice of location is acoustics:

'Today we tend to enter these caves speaking in hushed tones, but this may be wrong – the original artists or users of the caves may well have been singing, chanting, or praying loudly while the images were being made or used. We will never know, but on studies of acoustics in some Ice Age decorated caves have detected a correlation between the locations of decoration and those places where men's voices can best be heard.

Often, the areas with the best decoration have the best acoustics, while undecorated areas are totally flat in terms of sound quality. In view of the obvious intelligence of artists, it is extremely likely that, just as they took full advantage of the morphology of the cave and of particular rock shapes, so they would also have used any acoustic peculiarities. Anyone who has heard stalactites being played inside a deep, dark cave – they produce a soft marimba-like sound – will know how amazing the experience can be.

One of the characteristics of Ice Age cave art is the exploitation of undulations in walls ... and to gain a better idea of how these shapes would have appeared to Ice Age visitors, it is necessary to replicate the sources of light they would have used ... which I believe can take us the farthest into the minds and motivations of the artists.' [*Cave Art: A Guide to the Decorated Ice Age Caves of Europe*]

In April 2003, engravings and bas-reliefs were found on the walls and ceilings of some of the Creswell caves, an important find as it had previously been thought that no British cave art existed. The discoveries, made by Paul Bahn, Sergio Rippoll and Paul Pettitt, included an animal figure at first thought to be an ibex but later identified as a stag. Later finds included carvings on the ceiling of Church Hole Cave, the rarity of which made the site one of international importance.

'To this day the finds at Creswell Crags represent the most northerly finds in Europe. Their subject matter includes representations of animals including bison and, arguably, several different bird species. The engravers seem to have made use of the naturally uneven cave surface in their carvings and it is likely that they relied on the early-morning sunlight entering the caves to illuminate the art. The scientists and archaeologists concluded that it was most likely the engravings were contemporary with evidence for occupation at the site during the late glacial era around

13,000–15,000 years ago. Most of the engravings are found in Church Hole Cave on the Nottinghamshire side of the gorge. Since this discovery, however, an engraved reindeer from a cave on the Gower peninsula has yielded two minimum dates of 12,572 and 14,505 years.' [*Britain's Oldest Art:* The Ice Age cave art of Creswell Crags]

Not all of the figures identified as prehistoric art are in fact human made. An example given by archaeologists Paul Bahn and Paul Pettitt is the 'horse-head', which they say is 'highly visible and resembles a heavily maned horse-head... lacks any trace of work: it is a combination of erosion, black stains for the head, and natural burrow cast reliefs for the mane'. Others are a 'bison-head' which they think may be natural and a 'bear' image which 'lacks any evidence of human work'. Notwithstanding they believe that more figures may be discovered in the future.

We also now know that sound plays an important role in magical practice, and research into our ancient past is showing us very interesting technologies employed by ancient societies. Also, in history we see how the Greeks and Egyptians, and many other cultures worldwide used sound and light, and sometimes psychedelic substances in their temples. The very bluestones of Stonehenge – themselves a long way from their native Preseli mountains – were hewn from rocks that 'sing'.

Music is composed of three elements or threads that combine to create special vibrations that act and react on the ear, the consciousness and the soul. These three elements can be classed as rhythm, melody and harmony - and harmony is the basic ingredient of music. According to Dolores Ashcroft-Nowicki [*The Ritual Magic Workbook*],

'...harmony is the receptacle or Grail of music with rhythm as the vital essence or energy poured into the harmonic form. Melody organises these two basics into the finished product.

Music will, indeed must, be an integral part of temple work: the early church used music to great effect culminating in the beautiful Plainsong and Gregorian Chants. Although primarily Christian these chants can be used in many different rituals and traditions simply because they are specially designed to lift the consciousness onto another level'.

In prehistory, sound would have been perceived differently than it is today. At a time when stone buildings were rare, spaces with acoustics would have been wondrous to those who entered them. Dr. Rupert Till, a Senior Lecturer in Music Technology at the University of Huddersfield, suggests that most previous studies of Stonehenge focused on looking at the site, rather than listening to it. He came up with the theory that the famous ring of stone could have sung like a crystal wine glass with a wet finger rubbing the rim.

Caves have also influenced cultural story-telling and literature and Thomas Hardy hints at this in his novel *Tess of the D'Urbervilles*. Reading carefully between the lines with an acoustician's ear, one can find him discussing various acoustic effects. Further research turned up an interview with the author in which he states that 'if a gale of wind is blowing, the strange musical hum emitted by Stonehenge can never be forgotten'.

Caves have long been connected to various legends of 'sleepers'. In both Christian and Muslim tradition, the 'Seven Sleepers' is the story of a group of youths who hid inside a cave outside the city of Ephesus to escape a religious persecution and emerged some 300 years later. The Qur'an mentions a dog among the sleepers, who remains on guard in front of the opening of the cave, protecting them in their sleep; the dog was called Kytmyr.

'Thou wouldst have deemed them awake, whilst they were asleep, and We turned them on their right and on their left sides: their dog stretching forth his two fore-legs on the threshold: if thou hadst come up on to them, thou wouldst have certainly turned back from them in flight, and wouldst certainly have been filled with terror of them.' (Surah Al-Kahf, Qur'an: 18)

King Arthur's knights also took the rather drastic action of sealing themselves in a cave - now known as Ogof Llanciau Eryri, which translates to Cave of the Young Men of Snowdonia. After Arthur died, his surviving knights entered a cave below the summit of Y Lliwedd and the entrance was sealed behind them. It is said that the knights' slumber there still, fully armoured and armed, waiting for their king to awaken and fulfil the ancient prophesy that Arthur merely sleeps until Wales is in mortal danger, whereupon he will arise and save his country.

Nevertheless, this is obviously when the great awakening of symbolic, often referred to as religious, thought began. The mysterious painted caves point to the time when mankind began to probe the boundaries of spirituality and are the cathedrals that witnessed the birth of religious belief. Questions inevitably follow. How and why did the ancient artists do it? The underworld cathedrals of Palaeolithic times were dark, dangerous, dank and depressing. They had to crawl through small openings carrying some other sputtering light source, fully aware that if it went out, leaving them in darkness so profound they couldn't even see their hand in front of their face, they would probably die there. The sharp, ragged rocks scraped their back and knees, and unfathomable drop-offs opened up suddenly before them at every turn. They risked their life and sanity every time. Why would they do such a thing?

Chthonic might seem a lofty and learned word, but it's actually pretty down-to-earth in its origin and meaning, since comes from *chthōn*, which means 'earth' in Greek, and is associated with things that dwell in or under the earth. In his book *The Mycenaean World*, linguist and classicist John Chadwick argues that many chthonic deities may be remnants of the native pre-Hellenic religion. And yet within living memory, at the inconspicuous ancient Neolithic village of Carn Euny (Cornwall) there is a small, enclosed opening in the ground that leads to an underground chamber called a fogou. Back when this village was occupied it was necessary to go to quite a bit of trouble to reach this subterranean, human-constructed cave, crawling on hands and knees down into the darkness.

> 'But there would inevitably come a day when kids grew old enough to be initiated into adulthood. Suddenly mystery confronted them, and I imagine they were frightened out of their wits. Here was a whole unexplored realm, right beneath their feet. It must have been a spiritual awakening, discovering new worlds, adult worlds, and magical worlds where children were now expected to behave in a new way and take on mature responsibilities. What went on down here? What did they learn? What mysteries were revealed?'
> [*The Modern Antiquarian*]

There is no doubt many of these dark mini-caves all over the world serving a similar purpose. But once we get down on our hands and knees and make the mental and spiritual effort to crawl through the tunnel, we will, like the children of Carn Euny, never be the same again. We will discover a world where much is the same, only more so. We will discover the world of spirit, the world of alternate realities, the multi-verse, the place of alternative perceptions. It's right there underneath our feet but we'll never experience it unless we start searching …

Mystical Interlude: The Descent into the Cave Pathworking

When Stone Age man was moved to make the perilous descent into the caves of southern France and northern Spain, braving the dangerous passageways, bone-numbing cold, impenetrable darkness, and the complete and total silence for the purpose of painting the rock-face with magnificent images of the animal kingdom, he could never have foreseen that tens of thousands of years later men and women would view those hidden paintings and be awestruck by their majestic and mysterious beauty.

For this path-working we will be following the *Descent into the Cave* with Dr Ilse Vickers of University College London, who has been engaged in exploring the links between mythology, religion and the psyche, and in this connection, she is working on the dynamic relationship between depth psychology and Palaeolithic cave art. [The Bradshaw Foundation]

'We are far removed from the image makers of the Ice Age and it is impossible to say with any certainty what made them undertake these dark and dangerous journeys, or, indeed, what thoughts and beliefs motivated them to place the images in the innermost, darkest recesses of the caves. True, our consciousness is far more developed than that of our forebears and we may justifiably think of ourselves as modern. All the same, we cannot escape the fact that there is another life in us, one that from our higher but lopsided rational position we either cannot or no longer want to see: our prehistoric past. According to Jung, *'every civilized human being, however high his conscious development, is still an archaic man at the deeper levels of his psyche'*. This being the case, what is it then that distinguishes our psychology from that of Ice-Age man?'

For primitive man for whom *everything* was significant, the belief in the power of chance was entirely natural and logical. On the discovery of a deep cave he would have felt diminished and his response most likely would have been one of profound terror and of awe. Nor, it must be observed, is it only primitive man who responds in this way to the mystery of naturally created caves - at the deepest levels of our being we are still archaic and connected to the past - as the philosopher Seneca writing in the 1st century CE so eloquently reminds us:

'If ever you have come upon .... a cave, made by the deep crumbling of rocks, holds up a mountain on its arch, a place not built with hands but hollowed-out into such spaciousness by natural causes, your soul will be deeply moved by a certain intimation of the existence of God'.

According to Dr Vickers, many modern explorers of Palaeolithic caves have reported that when they had reached the extremes of the cave, that is, when they had reached a point where their intellectual navigational tools had become useless, they had suddenly found themselves under the spell of irrational fears, prompting atavistic feelings. Moreover, with their senses, as it were, switched off, it seemed to them that they were looking inwards as if seeing with an 'inner eye'. This, of course, is understandable, because a descent into the deep underground darkness is a journey to the remotest land where for the seeker with the right mind-set, the portal to Otherworld may be discovered.

'From a purely psychological point of view, one could describe the descent into the underground caverns as at once an actual, physical journey as well as an inner journey; the descent without corresponds to the descent within. With every step downwards, one travels back in time, sheds layer after layer of human history until one arrives at a mysterious place beyond duality and outside rational explanation. It is a place where all differentiations between the known and the intuitively felt become blurred, where one flows into the other, and miraculously becomes the other. Not surprisingly,

Jung described the psycho-physical journey as 'a blissful and terrible experience' - a hellish journey into the future.'

The paintings give a glimpse of eternity between two worlds, the finite and the infinite, the conscious and the unconscious. Put another way, we can see the visions as images of the divine made manifest in animal form. We are reminded of the archaic Mithraic mystery cult where the bull (*aurochs*) because of its inordinate, superhuman strength played such a central role. As the super, tutelary animal, the bull here (as in so many other myths) represents the great archetypal symbol for the primordial, eternal forces of creation rolling into time. In the underground Mithraeum there is always a chamber at the far end of which we find the tauroctony, an image of the god slaying the divine bull. The belief was that the sacrificial death of the bull-god would cause the re-birth of nature. [*The Power of the Bull*]

And staying with the Mystery cults of classical times, they were called 'mystery cults' not because they used mystical scripts or doctrines but because their rituals performed in underground sanctuaries promised to give the adept the *mysterious*, exalted experience of seeing the divine face to face, of becoming deified. As the experience could not be explained rationally, it was a carefully guarded taboo subject. Not much is therefore known of what actually took place during the celebration of the rites deep within in the caves. However, we do have one account in the form of a novel entitled *The Golden Ass* written by the Roman philosopher Apuleius, who wrote:

'I reached the boundary of death, ... and then I returned, carried through all the elements; in the middle of the night I saw the sun blazing with bright light; I approached the gods below and the gods above face to face, and worshipped them from nearby ...'

For this path-working we require darkness: the darkness of the cave ... the darkness of the tomb ... and silence. None are easy to find in our modern light-polluted, crowded world, so we must do the best we can as we begin with a long descent from the cave entrance into the gloom. After making ourselves comfortable (and with the aid of a blindfold if necessary), we begin by visualising the outer cave where diffused light can reach through a tangled curtain of ferns and other trailing plants; it is probably a fairly familiar environment but we are about to leave the security of the light and descend into darkness.

There are many images on the internet featuring bulls, bison, deer, mammoths, horses, rhinoceros, etc., of the Lascaux and Chauvet cave paintings and a study of these will help to set the scene prior to beginning the visualisation. Prehistoric artists used the earth pigments available in the vicinity: minerals limonite and hematite, red and yellow ochre and umber, charcoal from the fire (carbon black), burnt bones (bone black) and white from grounded calcite (lime white). By making a study of these images we can recreate them in our mind's eye for the Pathworking.

This is a world of touch because our hands follow the rough contours of the walls as we walk slowly sown a long tapering passageway that gets narrower and lower as we progress. Not knowing if a bottomless pit is about to appear at our feet. By using the descriptions given in the chapter, we begin crouching as we go deeper, then crawling on all fours, until we are wriggling down a narrow tube flat on our belly – deeper and darker – until the walls open out and releasing us from the close confinement of the rock. But we know we have come as far as we can go into the heart of the mountain and that there's still the long return journey to make...

Suddenly there is the barest glimmer of weak light, like that produced by a primitive oil lamp that is barely more than a large shell containing animal fat and a floating wick. In this dimly lit cavern, the gentle flicker of the flame reveals a host of brilliant creatures that have been painted onto the rock face in rich reds and black outlines. The flickering movement of the flame gives these massive animals breath as we slowly take in the images – long dead but very much alive when these paintings were made. These enormous beasts cover the walls and ceiling of the cavern like vast herds of animals sacred to the tribe, whose artists had hidden them away at the end of a long and arduous crawl where they were safe from prying eyes.

We stand in awe of this world of darkness that was never meant to be seen by ordinary eyes, when the flame begins to dim and slowly the images recede into the shadows, until once again the darkness gathers around us and we are alone in the silence. Fortunately for us, the path-working ends here and we do not have to make that slow, dangerous crawl back towards the light. But prior to leaving this sacred place we should spare a moment to pay homage to those unknown ancestors who created this magnificent sanctuary ... before stamping our feet and clapping our hands to break the spell, and where a flask of hot coffee and a sweet biscuit is waiting to bring us back to earth and 'ground' those magical energies.

This confining atmosphere also plays an important part in the ascetic disciplines of Shinto, and is called *komori*, meaning seclusion, preferably in the darkness of a cave. Like its association with the waterfall, the power-giving qualities of seclusion in darkness gestate and grow, 'until it bursts its covering and emerges into the world'. And here we remind ourselves of Chet Raymo's words that 'darkness is the mother of beauty, that extinction of light is a revelation ...' And he is right in his observation that few people willingly choose to walk the dark path, 'to enter the dark wood, to feel the knot of fear in the stomach, or to live in the black cave of the sleepless night. But then, unexpectedly the truth emerges. The light of the mind returns bearing extraordinary gifts'.

Chapter Three

Home of the Gods

Anthropological studies show that the worship of ancestors and mountains were once largely inseparable. Ancestral cults were enshrined in simply pointing at specific mountains and remembering the stories that were passed down throughout the generations, and an interconnected web between history, landscape, and culture was formed within the folklore of different peoples. Such as the Hindu belief that **Mount Kailash** in Tibet is never climbed for it is considered sacrilege to step on it; it is the final resting place for the souls of the dead and considered to be sacred in four religions: Bon, Buddhism, Hinduism and Jainism. Similarly, the large Buddhist cemetery placed on **Mount Koyasan** in Japan is a place of pilgrimage.

Sacred mountains can also provide an important piece of cultural identity, similar to the Armenian people regarding **Mount Ararat** in eastern Turkey to be the site of Noah's Ark of the Bible and, as a result, even people who do not live close to the mountain feel that events connected to it are relevant to their own personal lives. This results in communities banning certain activities near a mountain, especially if those activities are seen as potentially spiritually destructive to the sacredness itself. While according to the *Torah* (and consequently the Old Testament), **Mount Sinai** is the location where Moses received the Ten Commandments directly from God - the tablets forming the covenant - which is a central cornerstone of the three main Abrahamic faiths.

Mount Meru is the sacred five-peaked mountain of Hindu, Jain, and Buddhist cosmology and is considered to be the centre of all the physical, metaphysical and spiritual universes, and described to be one of the highest points on

Earth - the centre of all creation. In the Hindu religion, it is believed that Meru is home to the god Brahma, who is the father of the human race and all the demigods produced afterward. Indian cosmology believes that the sun, moon, and stars all revolve around Mount Meru, while folklore suggests the mountain rose up from the ground piercing the heavens giving it the moniker 'navel of the universe'.

In contemporary indigenous beliefs, various cultures around the world still maintain the importance of mountain worship and sacredness. The Taranaki people of New Zealand centred their whole life around **Mount Taranaki,** as well as taking their livelihood from its streams. The rivers that flowed down its steep terrain fed the flora and fauna, and gave the tribe all they needed for life. Life came from the mountain, and when life was taken away, it ultimately returned to the sacred slopes.

Similarly, Japan is one of the world's most mountainous countries, so it's not surprising that mountain worship is an historic element of Japanese culture. The mountains – **Haku, Tateyama,** and **Fuji** - Japan's three holy peaks were the sacred places that the mountain *Shugendo* creed used for worship since people believe that the force emanating from these mountains to be the source of life. The magnificent existence of the peaks is overwhelming to human beings due to their immensity and each of these three mountains is believed to have a particular power:

Mount Haku: The main peaks of this mountain are Gozengamine, Kengamine, and Ōnanjimine, while Mount Sannomine and Bessan are sometimes included to make the number of peaks to be five. There are several lakes close to Mount Haku's summit, which is why the mountain is said to have the power of water.

Mount Tateyama: Climbing to the mountain's top is said to be a simulation of the hell- paradise experience according to local belief and has made the mountain the source of spiritual power of the dead. The mountain is a source of two rivers – the

Hayatsuki and the Tsurugisawa - which both flow to the Sea of Japan.

Mount Fuji: Japan's most famous and highest mountain, has an exceptional symmetric cone shape which is the famous symbol that most photographs and arts of the region depict. The mountain also has snow covering at its top for around five months of the year. Mount Fuji, known as *Fuji-san*, is the sacred mountain of Japan with several Shinto temples at its base, all of which all pay homage to the mountain. A common belief is that *Fuji-san* is the incarnation of the earth spirit itself and the *Fuji-ko* sect maintains that the mountain is a holy being, and the home to the goddess Sengen-sama and the source of volcanic power.

In diverse cultures around the world, mountains are believed to be the realm of all sorts of entities and therefore deemed to be sacred - which may explain why many ancestral tombs are found in elevated places, looking out over the landscape. Beautiful and uplifting to the spirit, or barren, rocky and sinister, mountains have been widely regarded as being a source of inspiration and strength, so is it any wonder that they were conceived as the home of the ancestors? And where ancient man wanted to inter his own remains?

Mountains and hills have an extremely varied symbolism – a range of barren, jagged, towering peaks suggests primitiveness, difficulty and danger, illustrating the uncanny and ominous quality of mountain scenery. Other ranges are seen as pleasing and edifying to the spirit, emblems of the stable and eternal, and because they reach up from the earth towards the sky are symbols of the ascent from the earthly plane to the spiritual. The summits of prominent hills and mountains may have been symbolically important places to locate clan tombs, completing that final stage of a journey which took the deceased upwards through the roof of the burial chamber to the sky, where 'the dead, now revived, joined the cyclic Sun, and very likely, a god or gods associated with it in the eternal rounds of cosmological life, death and rebirth'.

'Such a proposition makes cultural sense in terms of why humans chose elevationally high places for ceremonial or burial purposes. Summits offer expansive views, are the interface between two worlds, and have a perceived proximity to the cosmic zone above. The crest of a hill or mountain is also a boundary that acts as an edge between the terrestrial world and the celestial domain. Such a perceived division suggests zoning, a process that humans may have used to rationalize the indeterminate division between the intangible 'above' and the familiar terrain below. Mountain summits forming distinctive profiles or notches when viewed from afar can also act as culturally meaningful targets for megalithic alignment.' [*Modern Archaeoastronomy: From Material Culture to Cosmology*]

Ascending from lowland to the summits of hills and mountains, where the majority of passage tombs are located, can provide us with a hands-on experience of an intangible 'other world'. In reality, landforms have not changed since Neolithic times and this provides an unchanging link with prehistoric people undertaking the same spiritual journeys. As we climb the slopes, our senses become acutely heightened due to the exposed nature of the location. Feelings of power provoked by topographical gradient, elevation, expansive views, and the almost tangible sense of being close to another domain, could partly answer the question as to why such locations were chosen for tomb-building purposes.

The research paper *Interpreting megalithic tomb orientation and siting within broader cultural contexts,* shows that the phenomenon was invariably located at a higher elevation on the skyline, suggesting a symbolic and hierarchical relationship in their relative placement in the landscape with additional astronomical declinations with an axial alignment towards the rising and setting positions of the sun at the Winter and Summer Solstices. However, Frank Prendergast claims that the analysis of prehistoric tomb orientations solely in terms of their axial alignment on rising/setting celestial targets is an arguably restrictive and culturally narrow perspective, and that some tomb entrances were deliberately orientated towards key focal places in the landscape.

Nevertheless, this perceived division between these two worlds - one above and the other below - may have been regarded as a transitional boundary, an intangible demarcation between such worlds. The 'above' is hostile, remote, mysterious and seemingly closer to the gateway to the afterlife. The 'below' is familiar, lived-in and understood. If such interpretations suggest liminality - that transitional phase of a rite of passage - then it could also serve as a basis to explain the link between mind and landscape. The dynamic of moving up or down a mountainside from one phase to another, is an experience that is sharpened by an indefinable but conscious state of passing through such a metaphysical threshold created in the mind by the beliefs of the people. The motivation to place them in such physically challenging and remote parts of the landscape most likely stem from the need to rationalise the worlds of everyday existence and the afterlife, which is consistent with the basic human necessity for balance and equilibrium in life.

For example, Pentre Ifan (Wales) dates from around 4,000-3500 BCE and is unusually oriented opening to the south, standing on the slope of a ridge commanding extensive views over the Nevern Valley and Fishguard Bay. What we see today is but a fragment of the original structure but the stones of the chamber are all of local igneous rock while on the portal stone there is a faint decorative cup-mark. It has also been noted that the slope of the dolmen's capstone echoes the angle of the Carn Ingli ridge visible on the western skyline. Carn Ingli was considered sacred up until early Christian times and harbours noteworthy magnetic anomalies. The striking, highly distinctive rock clusters known as Carnedd Meibion-Owen are visible precisely on the south-western skyline from Pentre Ifan. The stones marked a burial site that consisted of a number of burial pits. Further study revealed that the site may actually have been built during two separate time periods with the ancient burial chambers being installed first, followed by the larger standing stones, suggesting there may have been a further ritual purpose to the site.

At Duntreleague (Ireland) the long-range visibility of, and intervisibility between, many of the passage tombs in Ireland occurs as a result of their elevated skyline position; the name is derived from *Dún-Trí-Liag*, meaning the 'fort of three pillar stones'. The monument stands on a platform below the summit of Duntryleague Hill with the entrance passage facing north-west in line with the mid-summer sunset. It is one of many sites that can be found in the nearby woodland, all dating back some 4,000 years to the Bronze Age, signifying strong religious ritual dating back as far as 3,500 BCE. An unopened circular cairn crowns the summit of the hill while across the Glen of Aherlow to the south, is a conspicuous cairn, on the summit of Temple Hill that overlooks Duntryleague and the passage tomb at Shrough, which occupies a hilltop position on the northern side of the Glen.

Beyond the British Isles, *Interpreting megalithic tomb orientation* cited the orientation of Scandinavian passage tombs that suggested possible links with a sacred point/place far out in the landscape. While in a study of 81 dolmens in Bulgaria, used topographical analysis to show that axial orientation is significantly aligned towards distant prominent mountain peaks - while in the northern Sakar Mountains in the same region, some tombs are directed at other typologically similar monuments. In southwest Iberia, the largest Neolithic tomb in Europe (Cueva de Menga) is shown to be topographically aligned on a distant conspicuous peak, and provides evidence for a cluster of Neolithic dolmens in Central Portugal where a link between monuments of the region, a prominent mountain range and the rising of the bright star Aldebaran is argued and supported by local folklore.

In North America, the Navajo possess a strong belief system in regards to the natural-supernatural world and have a belief that objects have a supernatural quality and consider mountains to be sacred. There are four peaks, which are believed to have supernatural aspects. The mountains each represent a borderline of the original Navajo tribal land, including **Mount Taylor**, the **San Francisco Peaks**, **Blanca Peak**, and **Hesperus Peak** located in the La Plata Mountains. Each mountain peak is representative of a colour, direction, and correlates with a cultural light phenomenon dealing with the cosmic scheme of the rising and of the setting sun.

Directionally, the mountains are described in a clockwise motion following the movement of the sun beginning with the eastern mountain of Blanca Peak. Blanca Peak is associated with the colour white and the 'Dawn Man' referring to the rising of the sun. Next in the south is Mount Taylor, which is associated with the colour blue and the 'Horizontal Blue Man' referring to the daytime. In the west are the San Francisco Peaks, which represent the colour yellow and the 'Horizontal Yellow Woman' associated with the setting sun. And finally, in the north, is the Hesperus Peak which is given the colour black and belongs to the light phenomenon of the 'Darkness Woman' representing the night-time, according to 'Symbolic Elements in Navajo Ritual'. [*Southwestern Journal of Anthropology* Vol. 25 No. 3]

While **Mount Shasta**, located near the Oregon border in northern California, holds the distinction of being one of the world's pre-eminent sacred mountains. It is recognized as an eligible Native American cultural and cosmological property on the National Register of Historic Places. Artifacts found in the surrounding area suggest at least 11,000 years of human habitation, designating this region as one of the longest-occupied areas of North America. The mythic significance of Mount Shasta's vast antiquity places it on par, historically and categorically, with other sacred sites found among the world's oldest known civilizations, including the temples and pyramids of Egypt, Stonehenge, the Mayan pyramids, and Machu Picchu.

From a philosophical and spiritual standpoint, Mount Shasta is far more powerful and impressive than anything ever built by man. It is a Creator-made temple and monument, half a billion years old. In an abstract geological sense, it is still alive and under construction – and it will continuously erupt, regenerate, and change forms far into the future. Native Americans have observed Mount Shasta as a sacred mountain from time immemorial; they viewed the mountain and its surroundings as holy ground since it is thought to be one of the first earthly places created by the Great Spirit. In the past, no one but medicine men or women climbed up the mountain beyond the tree line. It was thought too powerful for ordinary people to visit, and inhabited by hosts of potentially dangerous spirits and guardians who could harm a person who traveled up the mountain unprepared.

A sacred mountain tends to possess unusual characteristics which are more than just the accumulation of natural processes. There is, we feel, something different about a sacred mountain which cannot be easily explained: something that makes it exceptional. It possesses a kind of energy that's unique to itself, which can be sensed and felt as much as seen. It draws people to it … inexplicably, mysteriously: 'The power of such a mountain,' writes Lama Anagarki Govinda,

'is so great and yet so subtle that without compulsion pilgrims are drawn to the mountain from near and far, as if by the force of some invisible magnet, and they will undergo untold hardships and privations in their inexplicable urge to approach and to worship the sacred spot. Nobody has conferred the title of sacredness upon such a mountain; by virtue of its own magnetic and psychic emanations the mountain is intuitively recognized to be sacred. It needs no organiser of its worship; innately, each of its devotees feels the urge to pay it reverence.'

All over the world there are places anciently known for their anomalous energies and mysterious phenomenon.

Today experts recognize that these 'sacred sites' influence human consciousness and other living organisms in a number of unusual and remarkable ways. They have become colloquially known as ancient 'power spots', places where people commonly experience unusual phenomenon such as UFO-related activity, portals into other dimensions, consciousness-altering experiences, and other paranormal-phenomenon. When one enters into a sacred site of so-called powerful energy, the mind, body, and spirit are instantly affected. The energy at these places can even be felt, sensed, dowsed, photographed, and measured with scientific instrumentation. The spiritual use of these major power spots is now beginning to be thought of as a unifying influence behind the rise of human civilization. Previously it was believed that spirituality arose only after mankind had already developed farming and villages, and religion was subsequently invented as a coercive means to promote social cooperation and control.

Mystical Interlude: Magical Crystals, Sacred Stones

Regardless of where we live in the world, some geological formations are better suited for magical or creative working than others, an idea that was mooted by Dion Fortune in her novel, *The Goat-Foot God*. ...

'Now the best place to get the kind of experiences you want is on chalk. If you think of it, all the earliest civilisation in these islands was on the chalk … Avebury's on the chalk; and St Albans is on the chalk …'

Christopher Tilley in *A Phenomenology of Landscape,* however, gives a wider overview of the topographic features of the prehistoric landscape that attracted our distant ancestors' attention: an affinity with the coast; mountain escarpments and spurs; the ridges, valleys and chalk downlands. Obviously, the most important aspect of each site being not what is seen above ground, but in the geological formation *beneath our feet.*

There are, of course, many different types of rock that make up the Earth's surface and each of them will have certain positive or negative magical/creative properties. As an example, we will look at what has been found to be the best and the worst when it comes to drawing from, or stifling magical/creative energy.

The Best: Slate is a widespread, metamorphic rock commonly found inter-layered with sedimentary strata and with rocks of volcanic origin. Once we understand that *quartz* is very abundant in slate and may form as much as 70% by weight of the rock, it is not difficult to see why this particular material generates so much Earth energy – quartz being one of the most powerful crystals on the planet. Magical, psychic and creative working on slate packs a very distinctive punch, especially if the slate layers are close to the surface.

The Worst: Clay - the name derives from Old English *clæg* meaning 'sticky' - is a widespread sedimentary rock with grains too small to be seen under any but the most powerful microscope, and may form in many different geological environments throughout the world. The most extensive layers are found in both deep and shallow marine deposits, in moraines (piles of debris) left behind by receding glaciers, and in zones of pre-existent rocks (especially granite) that have been altered by hydrothermal fluids. Try walking through heavy clay and it immediately becomes apparent why Earth energy is often 'blocked' or sluggish. Magical working on clay involves a lot of energy-generating techniques by the practitioner, and unless there is a considerable amount of experience (and knowledge) to draw on, things may take a long time to come to fruition.

Here in the Glen of Aherlow, however, the mountains are Old Red Sandstone – a tough enduring rock formed during the 'Caledonian Foldings', the mountain-building period of Earth's long history. The pressure caused the underlying softer Silurian rocks to fold into great ridges; and over millions of years the erosion dust compacted to form this magnificent range of Red Sandstone peaks. The Galtees are Ireland's highest inland mountain range, a high ridge which rises up almost sheer from the surrounding plain. Two major Ice Ages have affected the area, and the rounded summits of the Galtees are due to the higher parts being above the ice. This freeze-thaw action on the higher peaks gradually wore them away to form the stony, scree covered summits we see today. This glacial action also formed cirques (or corries) on the higher slopes – amphitheatres or hollows, which are now five gloomy lakes.

Despite being easily weathered, sandstone has been used by builders and sculptors for thousands of years, including the ancient ruins of Petra (Jordan), which has been described poetically, by John William Burgon, as 'a rose-red city half as old as time'. The disadvantages of sandstone are out-weighted by its natural beauty and the ease with which it can be shaped and carve into outstanding works of art such as the famous bust of Queen, Nefertiti that has survived more or less intact since it was carved during the Egyptian 18th Dynasty.

And as I observed in *Magic Crystals, Sacred Stones* and *The Hollow Tree: A beginner's guide to the Tarot and Qabalah*, because sandstone is highly susceptible to weathering and decomposition, and ultimately crumbling to dust, we can safely assign it to the Element of Earth. Or more precisely, the *'Earthy part of Earth'* symbolised by the Princess of Disks in the Tarot, who represents the 'element of the brink of Transfiguration'. She has been depicted with her sceptre descending into the Earth where the point becomes a diamond, and her shield denoting the 'twin spiral forces of Creation in perfect equilibrium'. The Element of Earth is directed towards the North and the 'Place of Power'.

The energies of the Glen *are* 'dark' – not in any negative sense – but because the primitive history of the place is unchanged and unchanging just like in my homeland of Wales, near the Preseli Mountains. Those hills are also dotted with prehistoric remains, including evidence of Neolithic settlement, and in 1923 the bluestone from those hills was identified with that used to build the inner circle of Stonehenge. Archaeologists have since pinpointed the precise place from where the bluestones were removed in about 2500 BCE - a small crag-edged enclosure at one of the highest points of the Carn Menyn mountain. The stones were then moved 240 miles to the famous site at Salisbury Plain.

'Bluestone' is the common name for spotted dolerite, an igneous rock that looks blue when broken and is spotted with small pellets of feldspar and other minerals that got into the molten matrix when the rocks were forming geological ages ago. While the particular reasoning and importance behind this choice of rock remains unknown, it was clearly justified by the considerable effort that was required to move it – it has been suggested that the dolerite stones may also have been selected because of their acoustic qualities.

A recent study shows that rocks in the Preseli Mountains have a sonic property where thousands of stones along the ridge were tested and a high proportion of them were found to 'ring' when they were struck. 'The percentage of the rocks on the Carn Menyn ridge are ringing rocks, they ring just like a bell,' said researcher

Paul Devereux, the principal investigator on the Landscape and Perception Project. 'And there are lots of different tones ... you could play a tune. In fact, we have had percussionists who have played proper percussion pieces off the rocks.' According to Devereux, the discovery of the 'resonant rocks' could explain the reason why they were selected for Stonehenge. 'There had to be something special about these rocks,' he said. 'Why else would they take them from here all the way to Stonehenge?'

And quartz was sometimes used to embellish an external façade/wall or pavement at the entrance of these Neolithic monuments. In the case of the tomb at Newgrange, whether quartz was originally and exclusively used to decorate the entire front of the cairn, or was laid as a pavement, is a matter of continuing discussion. Either way, the visually striking exterior is seen as being an architectural threshold that demarcated and emphasised the separation between the world of the living and the realm of the dead – and quartz as we know has amazing magical and mystical qualities.

- Once you have located what appears be a suitable site, try to pinpoint your own personal energy spot by using a pendulum that contains an element of quartz. Dowse the site thoroughly and calculate where the energy is the strongest from the pendulum's reaction.

- If a location seems unsuitable for magical or inspirational working, then a short journey might make all the difference. For example: the short distance between the clay plain levels at Charnwood and the granite outcrop was only a daily dog's walk away from each other.

The surrounding landscape *does* influence the way magical and creative workings come to fruition, and also the amount of effort needed to be put into the ritual or project to bring about the desired effect. By understanding what lies beneath our feet will enhance our magical and creative abilities, especially if we can learn to plug-in to the natural energy of the place.

Chapter Four

The Spiritual Ascent

'The white-clad wandering Japanese Yamabushi monks are mysterious, mystical figures, known for their magical abilities and contact with supernatural spirits and deities. Far away from civilization they practice their methods of training called *Shugendo* (magical powers through trial). These secret methods of spiritual attainment involve meditation training, sutras, pilgrimage and hardships that most mortals couldn't bear - standing under freezing waterfalls, walking on hot coals, fasting for days on end, learning to overcome the pain of chilli and mustard smoke in confined spaces. The monks are known for amazing feats such as being able to sit in a cauldron of boiling water, run up ladders made of sword blades and being able to spend up to seven days without food or water, or walk for 1000 days without a rest. They are said to be able to travel in the spirit to different realms. The Yamabushi live in total harmony with nature and with the spirits of nature called *Kami*.' [*Shugendo: The Way of the Mountain Monks*]

The cult evolved during the seventh century from an amalgamation of beliefs, philosophies, doctrines and ritual systems drawn from local folk-religious practices, pre-Buddhist mountain worship, Shinto, Taoism and esoteric Buddhism. *Shugendō* literally means 'the path of training and testing' or 'the way to spiritual power through discipline'.

The **Three Mountains of Dewa** refer to the three sacred mountains of Haguro, Gassan and Yudono, which are clustered together in the ancient province of Dewa. Holy to the Shinto religion and especially the mountain ascetic cult of *Shugendo*,

Dewa Sanzan is a popular pilgrimage site visited by many, including famed *haiku* poet Matsuo Bashō.

The Dewa Sanzan mountains are particularly noteworthy as having the oldest history of mountain worship in Japan. The mountains were first opened as a religious centre over 1400 years ago in 593 by prince Hachiko, who devoted his life to religious pursuits, eventually enduring difficult ascetic exercises and a period of penance, which led to his worship of Haguro Gongen, the deity of the mountain. Following this, the prince began worship at the Gassan and Yudono mountains, which led to the enshrinement of all three deities at the temple located on the summit of Mount Haguro.

Following the establishment of the Dewa Sanzan mountains as a centre of ascetic religious beliefs, many people began to make yearly pilgrimages to the mountains to pay reverence, even arduously trekking thousands of miles to visit the shrines during the summer months. These pilgrimages hold significance for many religions and the mountains served as a place of learning for various belief systems, but were most particularly important to *Shugendō*.

Graceful Mount Gassan has been a sacred mountain since the most ancient of times and its huge boulders and striking rock formations have long been thought to have miraculous powers. Mount Yudono likewise has sacred reddish-brown boulders, while Mount Haguro is noted for its old-growth trees and deep, ancient forests. Since prehistoric times Japanese nature worship has been based on the belief that spirits reside in everything, from mountains and seas to trees and rocks, and the three mountains of Dewa are prime examples of how this belief has been preserved through the centuries.

Each of the three mountains has its own shrine: Gassan Shrine, Yudonosan Shrine, and Ideha Shrine (on top of Mount Haguro). Because the Gassan and Yudonosan shrines cannot be accessed in winter when their tall mountains are covered in deep snow, there is a special collective shrine dedicated to the gods of all three mountains in the grounds of Haguro's Ideha Shrine. This collective shrine is called the *Sanjingōsaiden* in homage to the mystic wonder that enthralled the ancient mountain ascetics.

Folk religion has continued throughout the ages to be a very major force in the life of the Japanese people, particularly the aspect of the association between religious beliefs and practices with sacred mountains. This practice of mountain worship has become widespread throughout Japan's history and nearly every high mountain top has had its own dedicated shrine at some point, with some receiving pilgrimages every year from thousands of worshippers. This collection of diverse phenomena linking religious activities and beliefs with sacred mountains is referred to as *sangaku shinkō*.

Nevertheless, Mount Yudono is viewed as being the heart of the three sacred mountains and is considered the most holy of ascetic disciplinary practice grounds. Many ascetics and *yamabushi* believe they have not completed their pilgrimage, and thus entered the holy land, until they have reached Mount Yudono. Mount Yudono is famous for its *goshintai,* a sacred object believed to be directly connected to a god. The shrine on Yudono is also revered as hallowed land which must be kept secret, and even today, photography and video recordings are prohibited.

Mountains then, have a special spiritual significance for both the living and the dead – and if both leave an imprint upon the physical landscape, they also leave an indelible impression upon the landscape of our soul. But what is the relevance of traditional religion in a world enshrined in the rocks forced upwards to become misty mountains and towering cliffs? Taking his cue from the poet Gerard Manley Hopkins, who loved the natural world and saw it shot through with 'the grandeur of God', Chet Raymo also delves into the mystery of the universe and finds 'glimmers of the Absolute in every particular'. In the realm of the mystics and the spiritual practice of wonder he champions the cause of *When God Is Gone, Everything Is Holy* by encouraging us to wonder at the presence of an enchanted universe infused with mystery.

Raymo's approach to spiritual naturalism combines mundane and spiritual ways of looking at the world but with a hefty dollop of science thrown into the mix. Because how can knowing and understanding how the mountains were formed via the services of tectonic plate movement millions of years ago make them any the less sacred? In fact, followers of spiritual naturalism *are* generally scientifically-oriented in most aspects, with their primary difference from other naturalists being that the abandonment of superstition does not necessarily entail the abandonment of spirituality.

Here we find the intellectual and emotional experience of something greater than 'oneself' is seen as a phenomenon of enduring value; spirituality may be seen as 'an emotional response to reality' – while magical practitioners see the exploration and exploitation of natural energies as 'magical reality'. Neither should it be at odds with contemporary pagan beliefs since its adherents believe that nature, in all its diversity and wonder, is 'sufficient unto itself in terms of eliciting the intellectual and emotional responses' associated with spiritual experience, and that there is no need for faith in the traditional anthropomorphic concept of 'god' or similar ideas.

Pre-history is a peculiar place. It is beyond history ... and, in truth, beyond 'reality'. We can understand that a belief in 'god' allowed ancient peoples to attribute myths, legends and taboos to certain places, like mountains. The idea of a hidden god in common in many traditions – often hidden to the point of inaccessibility. The mystic and the scientist have this in common: they both seek the same deeply hidden essence of creation, and, by and large, are equally content that much of what they seek remains unknown. Mystic and scientist live at the portal between knowledge and mystery – between the commonplace and the divine. And yet ... since ancient times, sacred sites have had a mysterious allure for billions of people across the globe. Legends and contemporary reports tell of extraordinary experiences people have had while visiting these places. Different sacred sites have the power to heal the body, enlighten the mind and inspire the heart. What is the key to the mystery of the sacred sites and how can we objectively explain their power?

Nevertheless, as anthropologist Christopher Tilley observes in *A Phenomenology of Landscape*, an exclusively modernist Western logic has simply become superimposed on the past. In the process how many people have perceived the landscape in which they live as either irrevocably lost, or irrelevant, or both. Cultural meanings are only unimportant for those who choose to make them so. Science does not destroy belief – it strengthens it by removing superstition and allowing us to confront reality. Or as Chet Raymo reminds us: *When 'god' is gone everything is holy.*

Mystical Interlude: Place of Power or Sacred Site?

'It doesn't take much to stimulate the human body's electro-magnetic circuitry, in fact a small change in the local environment is enough to create a change in awareness and people who visit ancient temples and megalithic sites often describe such a sensation. The standard explanation is that such feelings are nothing more than a 'wow' factor - an endorphin rush - the result of visual stimuli from the overwhelming impression generated by megalithic constructions. But the cumulative evidence proves otherwise: that many ancient sacred places are actually attracting, storing, even generating their own energy fields, creating the kind of environment where one can enter an altered state of consciousness.' [*Ancient Origins*]

There is also the amazing phenomenon of the Adams Calendar in Mozambique where not only are each of the stone circles uniquely designed and astrologically aligned, those who designed the structures knew that the core of the earth itself rings like a bell, which produces energy; and when building these stone circles, certain rocks were used that also ring like bells and produce a special energy force. Each stone was placed according to the sound it made in relation to another, as well as the precise astrological position. The latest and most interesting discovery of the stone circles is the sound frequencies of the rock formations from the earth *beneath* them. With modern technology scientists have been able to detect and measure incredible sound frequencies with acoustic properties coming from the earth inside the circles that conduct electricity. These sound frequencies are shaped as flowers of sacred geometry as they rise to the surface. They also measured electronic fields 200 metres underground with a heat of up to eighty degrees Celsius - as hot as volcanic earth - inside the circles. There is no scientific explanation for this effect because there is no active volcano, and the temperature drops dramatically when measured from *outside* the circle - which is also unexplainable. [*Starchild*]

During the 1980s the Dragon Project, a comprehensive engineering study was undertaken to locate magnetism in sacred sites and the test site was the Rollright Stones in England. A magnetometer survey of the site revealed how a band of magnetic force is attracted into the stone circle through a narrow gap of stones that act as the entrance. The band then spirals towards the centre of the circle and one of the circle's western stones was also found to pulsate with concentric rings of alternating current, resembling ripples in a pond. The average intensity of the geomagnetic field *within* the circle was significantly lower than that measured outside, as if the stones acted as a shield.

Recent study of energy fields in and around Avebury, the world's largest stone circle, reveals how its megaliths are designed to attract a ground current *into* the site and how its circular ditch breaks the transmission of ground current and conducts electricity *into* the ditch, in effect concentrating energy and releasing it at the entrance to the site, sometimes at double the rate of the surrounding land. Magnetic readings at Avebury die away at night to a far greater level than can be accounted for under natural circumstances. They charge back at sunrise, with the ground telluric current from the surrounding land attracted to the henge just as magnetic fluctuations of the site reach their maximum. The effect of sacred sites behaving like concentrators of electromagnetic energy is enhanced by the choice of stone. Often moved across enormous distance, the stone used in megalithic sites contains substantial amounts of magnetite. The combination makes temples behave like weak, albeit huge, magnets.

Freddy Silva's article for Ancient Temple website [*They're Alive! Megalithic Sites Are More Than Just Stone*] shows how these energies can have a profound effect on the human body, 'particularly the dissolved iron that flows in blood vessels, not to mention the millions of particles of magnetite floating inside the skull, and the pineal gland, which itself is highly sensitive to geomagnetic fields, and whose stimulation begins the production of chemicals such as pinolene and serotonin, which in turn leads to the creation of the hallucinogen DMT. In an environment where geomagnetic field intensity is decreased, people are known to experience psychic and shamanic states'.

An exhaustive investigation has also been undertaken at the Carnac region of France, where some 80,000 megaliths are concentrated, revealing a similar phenomenon at work. Pierre Mereux's study of Carnac shows how its dolmens amplify and release underground currents throughout the day, with the strongest readings occurring at dawn.

'The dolmen behaves as a coil or solenoid, in which currents are induced, provoked by the variations, weaker or stronger, of the surrounding magnetic field. But these phenomena are not produced with any intensity unless the dolmen is constructed with crystalline rocks rich in quartz, such as granite.'

His readings of menhirs reveal an energy that pulsates at regular intervals at the base, positively-and negatively-charged, up to thirty-six feet from these upright monoliths, some of which still show carvings of serpents.

The composition of the stones and their ability to conduct energy should not be lost on someone with occult training since being very high in quartz, the specially chosen rocks are piezoelectric, which is to say they generate electricity when compressed or subjected to vibrations. The megaliths of Carnac, positioned as they are upon thirty-one fractures of the most active earthquake zone in France, are in a constant state of vibration, making the stones electromagnetically active! It demonstrates that the menhirs were not planted on this location by chance, particularly as they were transported from 60 miles (97 km) away, because their presence and orientation is in direct relationship to terrestrial magnetism.

'Ancient Mysteries traditions around the world share one peculiar aspect: they maintain how certain places on the face of the Earth possess a higher concentration of power than others,' Silva continues. 'These sites, named 'spots of the fawn' by the Hopi, eventually became the foundation for many sacred sites and temple structures we see today. What is interesting is that each culture maintains that these special places are connected with the heavens by a hollow tube or reed, and by this umbilical connection the soul is capable of engaging with the Otherworld during ritual. However, it also allows a conduit for the spirit world to enter this physical domain ...' [*Ancient Origins*]

Chapter Five

The Ring of Fire

History has seen some monstrous eruptions of volcanoes, from Mount Pinatubo's weather-cooling burp to the explosion of Mt. Tambora, one of the tallest peaks in the Indonesian archipelago. The power of such eruptions is measured using the Volcanic Explosivity Index (VEI) a classification system developed in the 1980 that's somewhat akin to the magnitude scale for earthquakes. The scale goes from 1 to 8, and each succeeding VEI is 10 times greater than the last. There haven't been any VEI-8 volcanoes in the last 10,000 years, but human history has seen some powerful and devastating eruptions. [*Live Science*]

From prehistoric times to, more recently, the pyrotechnics of the USA's **Mount St Helens**, volcanic eruptions have aroused fear and inspired myths. Often cultures have seen active volcanoes as the abode of gods - typically gods quick to anger. 'I think the creation of myths is essentially the human reaction to witnessing a natural process that you cannot explain,' says Haraldur Sigurdsson, a volcanologist at University of Rhode Island. 'So you attribute it to supernatural forces and you say it is a battle between the giants and the gods.'

But divine petulance aside, these traditional oral tales can contain valuable information about the type, and nature of volcanic eruptions. In particular they can contribute 'missing data' to geologists about events that happened hundreds or thousands of years ago. 'After 30 years of research in the geosciences I believe that the analysis of myths is hugely important,' Patrick Nunn explains. 'It can help bridge the gap between geological theory and human history and lead to scientific insights.'

Active volcanoes are located all across the planet. Many of these sites are located far from any sizable population and pose minimal risks to human activity, however, a few of these magma cones can be found near large urban areas and thus pose a high risk for catastrophic destruction should they experience a large eruption. The following are the most potentially destructive volcanoes that can be found on the so-called Pacific 'Ring of Fire'. So named for the numerous volcanoes that line the rim of the Pacific Ocean, the Ring of Fire is considered by scientists to be the most seismically active region on the planet.

Shaped more like a horseshoe than a Ring, overall, 75% of Earth's seismic activity (volcanoes and earthquakes) occurs within this belt. A string of 452 volcanoes stretches from the southern tip of South America, up along the coast of North America, across the Bering Strait, down through Japan, and into New Zealand. Several active and dormant volcanoes in Antarctica, however, complete the ring. Most of the active volcanoes on The Ring of Fire are found on its western edge, from the Kamchatka Peninsula in Russia, through the islands of Japan and Southeast Asia, to New Zealand.

Mount Fuji: Since Japan has over 100 active volcanoes, modern-day volcanologists have a lot to watch and worry about. High on the list of dangerous volcanoes is the Empire of the Sun's most notable landmark, and although this mountain last erupted on 16th December 1707, it is long overdue for an eruption. Some scientists are concerned that a large earthquake could trigger this mountain into a spectacular and deadly blast – so perhaps it is understandable that modern Japanese continue to make propitious offerings and prayers to their unpredictable neighbour.

Sakurajima: While Mount Fuji sits quiet, Sakurajima volcano in southern Japan is a very active mountain that has erupted many times in the last hundred years. The volcano occupies the peninsula in the centre of Kagoshima Bay, which was formed by the explosion and collapse of an ancient predecessor of today's volcano, which has been in near continuous eruption since 1955. It is said that Sakurajima gets its name from a beautiful goddess. This divine being was worshipped as a symbol of delicate earthly life - but there is nothing delicate about the cantankerous volcano that has inherited the goddess's name.

Krakatua: Known as 'The Fire Mountain' during Java's Sailendra dynasty, with records of seven eruptive events between the 9th and 16th centuries. Indonesia is famous for its island volcano, which blew up in 1883, killing tens of thousands, while also creating a world-wide change in weather that lasted for over a year. Even though *Anak Krakatua*, the Son of Krakatua, is back and should be watched, the greatest peril in this island nation could come from a volcano named, **Merapi.** Meaning 'Mountain of Fire', Merapi burst into flames in 2010, killing 350 people and leaving hundreds of thousands homeless.

Taal: Like many Pacific nations, the Philippines are a collection of many islands, most of which are home to some sort of volcano. Perhaps the scariest is Taal, which has a large lake nestled in the bowl of its caldera. Located on the main island of Luzon, Taal happens to be located near some substantial urban areas. If a major eruption should occur in the near future, the lake water could mix with the red-hot lava, creating an even more massive and deadly explosion. Taal volcano's appeal is otherworldly. It has an ethereal aura and its famed beauty is believed to come from an old saga that tells of a wise old man and the town of people he tried to guide.

Mayon: Also situated on Luzon next to the Gulf of Albay in a populated area on the southeast corner of the island. Since the area is heavily populated, eruptions from Mayon have to be watched carefully, especially since this volcano has been very active in the 21st century. The myth of the creation of Mayon volcano is as fiery as the heart of the peak itself, with a plot involving star-crossed lovers, and a tragic ending leading to the rise of the jewel of Albay.

Mauna Loa: Though Kilauea volcano on the main island of Hawai'i is currently in a state of eruption, it is not generally considered to be the most dangerous volcano on these Pacific islands. That honour goes to Mauna Loa – home of Pele, the goddess of fire who is said to live in Kilauea that sits on the flank of the huge Mauna Loa volcano. Legend has it that she is agreeable enough if respected, but woe be to anyone who takes her rocks or otherwise disrespects her. In general, Hawaiian volcanoes produce slow-moving lava flows that can destroy homes and also emit poisonous sulphur dioxide gas. What scientists worry about most are possible earthquakes and tsunamis triggered by an unusually large eruption.

Popocatépetl: Not all the dangerous volcanoes are located in Asia, for there are quite a few in Latin America, where dense population patterns of settlement mirror that of Asia. From Mexico to Chile, there are located many of these 'hot-spots'. Only fifty-miles southeast of Mexico City stands a towering, active, and once snow-covered volcano, called Popocatépetl. The loss of its snow cap is more likely due to an increase in volcanic activity rather than a sign of climate change. In Aztec mythology, the volcanoes were once two star-crossed lovers, the young brave warrior Popocatepetl and the beautiful princess Iztaccihuatl, whose silhouette many still be seen represented by the peaks.

Santa Maria: In 1902, this volcano awoke from a long sleep and killed at least 5,000 people with a violent eruption. Since that time much minor activity has occurred, but fortunately, nothing that has harmed the local population. Still, Santa Maria should be watched closely because another major volcanic event could occur at any time. According to folklore of the Guatemalans, the Santa Maria is the 'mother volcano' and her child is the Santiaguito volcano. Although there is no historical record of activity at Santa María prior to 1902, Cakchiquel Indian legend does refer to grand eruptions of the volcano, which was known in ancient times as Gagxanul - the naked volcano.

Arenal: South from Guatemala, it seems that every Latin America country that borders the Pacific Ocean has at least one major volcano that dominates the national psyche with its sheer physical presence, as well as an ongoing threat to explode without warning. In Costa Rica, it is the Arenal volcano, while in Nicaragua, it is the Momotombo volcano, overlooking Lake Managua. And in El Salvador, a tiny country filled with many volcanoes there are numerous candidates, such as the San Miguel or Santa Ana volcano.

Galeras: Running south from Columbia south to Chile, the Andes Mountains of South America are also home to numerous active volcanoes. These towering mountains that form the backbone of the South American continent were created when the vast Pacific plate collided with the South America plate. The result is a long range of mountains, home to numerous volcanic hot spots. The Galeras volcano in Columbia is considered one of the most dangerous in the region. With numerous small to medium sized eruptions in the past fifty years, along with a large nearby urban area of Pasto, this volcano could again explode creating a dire situation in the nearby city.

Cotopaxi: Unfortunately, this situation is mirrored further south in Ecuador, where the capital, Quito, sits in a large valley, adjacent to another active 20,000-foot volcano. This mountain is named Cotopaxi and has long been a geological hot spot in the Andes. Most recently in 2015, Cotopaxi showed signs that it was becoming more active and could again produce a major eruption.

Across the Pacific Ocean, on a clear day, Mount Shasta can be seen from over 100 miles away and is part of the thousand-mile-long Cascade Range stretching from northern California to British Columbia; one of the largest strato-volcanoes in the world, rising to an altitude of 14,179 feet; it is also part of the chain encompassing the Pacific Basin's notorious 'Ring of

Fire', along which the majority of the planet's earthquakes and eruptions occur.

North-western Californian Native American tribes traditionally view Mount Shasta as being connected to a wide range of important volcanic landscapes and mountains that extend northwards and southwards in their tribal territories. A primordial spiritual connection is believed to link all these energetically powerful sites together, including Mount Shasta, Lassen Peak, Lava Beds, Medicine Lake Highlands, Crater Lake, as well as many other lesser landmarks found throughout the region. There are many tangible and intangible qualities which make a mountain sacred, and some of these qualities go beyond its mere appearance. Mount Shasta isn't the tallest mountain in the west, but it is the most legendary.

Geologists consider Mount Shasta to be a very dangerous, high threat volcano; someday it will wake up and erupt again, possibly during this century. A volcanic eruption from Mount Shasta could match or exceed the scale of the 1980 eruption of Mount St. Helens. The effects of an eruption on the surrounding towns close to the base of the mountain are predicted to be catastrophic, and because volcanoes stay active for years after an eruption, the region may have to be closed off to the public for a very long time. Mount Shasta's fuse is already burning, and experts all agree, it's not a matter of *if* Mount Shasta will erupt again but *when*...

European volcanic history

Perhaps one of the oldest myths of mankind is that of Atlantis - the story about a prosperous kingdom that disappeared without trace. As the story goes, the people in this utopian civilization enraged the gods so much with their moral corruption that the deities sent one terrible night of fire and earthquakes. These catastrophes sank Atlantis into the ocean, never to be found. Plato told this moral tale and for centuries scholars have debated whether those events were true, or invented, and what the location of Atlantis might have been.

One incident that bears a striking similarity to the story was the massive volcanic eruption of the island of Santorini in the Aegean Sea near Greece about 3,600 years ago. The highly advanced civilization of Minoans who lived on the island disappeared about the same time. The eruption itself inspired the Greek poet Hesiod to write the poem *Theogony* in around 700BC, which described the battle of giants and gods on Mount Olympus.

'I started to become interested in the myth of Atlantis and the poem *Theogony* because these are our only written or only documented descriptions or interpretations of this huge volcanic phenomenon,' volcanologist, Haraldur Sigurdsson wrote. 'We don't have any other accounts so, if you accept that they are related to this event, then they do give you some information that you otherwise wouldn't have.' Several studies support the theory that the volcanic disaster of Plato's story of Atlantis relates to the Santorini eruption. 'And once archaeologists began to dig on Santorini they looked to the legend as a form of validation of what they were finding,' says John Dvorak, a geoscientist at the University of Hawaii.

Today, Italy is the most volcanically active country in Europe. It hosts three active volcanoes – Etna, Vesuvius and Stromboli – **Mount Etna**, the most active volcano in Europe, is "unstable and full of energy," and according to new reports, Etna – an active and mercurial volcano in Sicily – has produced a fresh eruption from a brand-new fissure. The southeast flank of Etna in is sliding towards the sea at a rate of several centimetres a year. Research published in *Science Advances* presents strong evidence that the slide isn't caused by pressure from magma inside the volcano but by gravity pulling on Etna's lower underwater slopes, far from the summit. The researchers emphasise that this means Etna is more susceptible to catastrophic collapse than had previously been realised, and that the same might be true of other coastal and island volcanoes.

Vesuvius, of course, is famously known for the eruption that destroyed the ancient cities of Pompeii and Herculaneum in the Gulf of Naples that was witnessed and documented by Pliny the Younger, a Roman administrator and poet. Mount Vesuvius was formed by the collision of African and the Eurasian tectonic plates and is one of the world's most dangerous volcanoes. Since the devastating 79 CE eruption, the 4,000-foot volcano has blown its top many times - most recently in 1944 - but none have been as powerful. A recent series of thirty-four earthquakes in one day have been recorded near Vesuvius, sparking fears that the volcano could be about to blow.

As long as there have been historical records, **Stromboli** has been constantly active, which makes it almost unique among the volcanoes in the world. Stromboli is a small island in the Tyrrhenian Sea, off the north coast of Sicily and part of the Calabrian Arc associated with the subduction of the African tectonic plate under the Eurasian plate. It is one of the most active volcanoes on Earth since it has been erupting almost continuously since 1932 – and because it has been active for much of the last 2,000 years with eruptions visible for long distances at night, it is known as the 'Lighthouse of the Mediterranean'. The grand finale of Jules Verne's novel *Journey to the Centre of the Earth* (1864) takes place on Stromboli.

And as a footnote: Napoleon's historic defeat at Waterloo may have been spurred by a volcano that erupted two months earlier, and nearly 8,000 miles away. During the decisive battle on 18th June 1815, the heavy rainfall that flooded Europe during May and June that year may have resulted from a significant atmospheric disturbance in April, when the Indonesian volcano Mount Tambora erupted.

Early attempts to explain volcanic activity sound much like myths to modern day scientists. The ancient Greeks believed volcanoes came from the release of compressed air inside mountains, much like a monstrous belch. The Romans took a more engineering approach in their explanations: they blamed eruptions on chemical reactions and underground compounds catching fire. 'They were trying to attribute what they saw to natural processes rather than to extra-terrestrial or godly activity,' Sigurdsson says. 'They were moving away from myths and moving toward realism.'

But myths, plus the belief in divine retribution, still prevail. After the 1980 eruption of Mount St. Helens in the US, two local Christian priests announced that the volcano had erupted because people had not been charitable enough and were not taking proper care of their families. 'Even in the most highly technical society, people are still trying to grasp meaning in that way,' John Dvorak says.

So, while science can't provide all the answers, maybe people still need myths to make sense of the senseless and to claw some meaning from the mayhem. Maybe myths provide a valuable tool for coming to terms with destruction and disaster, or living under a constant umbrella of uncertainty. So even in this age of advanced science and technology, myths still have their place. Myths can provide meaning and the rituals they inspire can provide comfort and a sense of security, as John Dvorak says. 'Myths and rituals help people cope with disaster, albeit in a very different way.'

Mystical Interlude: Threshold Between the Worlds

Protruding largely (and sometimes ominously) out from an otherwise unassuming landscape, volcanoes remind us of the goals we aspire to reach, the journey to get there, and the value of the climb to the top. Nevertheless, a volcano can also represent anger, vengeance, revenge, hidden emotions, destruction and unpredictable situations in our waking life. Predominantly, volcanoes reveal the incorporation of all the Elements, and as such hold an important symbolic power as they encompass the power of Earth, Air, Water and Fire. [*Symbolic Meanings*]

Earth: As an earth symbol (or the Earthy part of Fire) the volcano has long held its place in the Western world as a metaphor used to understand creation, morality, and nature itself. For instance, it is easy to see how the volcano is universally acknowledged as a thing of power in the natural world. The containment of gas and lava coupled with its release in violent eruption has become a general metaphor used to describe explosion in human life, whether this is of a personal, cultural or political nature.

Air: When we recognize the symbolism of air (or the Airy part of Fire) as a method of communication or thought – we can clearly identify how the symbolic smoke of our efforts demonstrate how artistic form can follow formlessness, and indeed, this concept is explored in both art theories and ancient cosmogonies. If the volcano is the image of the cosmos, so too it is the artist or creator who brings form to the cosmos and creates the world according to his own design. Contained within these actions is the great power for both creation and destruction.

Water: A symbol of water (or the Watery part of Fire) is found in the form of flowing lava in symbolic volcano fact and lore. In fact, volcanoes erupt because partial melting in the earth's mantle separates liquid and solid rock according to density; liquid rock or magma is less dense than solid rock and so it has a buoyancy that allows it to rise. This buoyancy in combination with the various pressures and caused by tectonic activity allow magma to break through the surface of the Earth. Eruptions change the faces of volcanic craters. Lava displaces rock and creates them at the same time. Volcanic activity can never be entirely predicted, and a volcano that has been quiet for a thousand years can suddenly decide to erupt violently destroying cities, or simply let off a cloud of steam that alerts scientists to monitor its activities.

Fire: Lastly as a fire symbol (or the Fiery part of Fire) volcanoes speak to us of passion, action, creativity and power. This mystery of the volcano, this 'sight epiphany', is perhaps why volcanoes have long been used as metaphors to express colossal power and fiery infernos, and were also at the heart of the 19th-century craze for the sublime, or that which is so immense that it is beyond human comprehension. The volcano, with its active, living spirit of magma (Fire), gas (Air), steam (Water) and rock Earth – not to mention the beauty and terror inspired by such natural activity, spark the imagination of the artist.

But it is in Greek and Roman mythology that the metaphor of the volcano first becomes manifest in the Western canon of religious and philosophical thought, and it is here that the symbols in the unconscious mind takes on a more complicated form. Beyond symbols, Jung argues that basic motifs in the human mind become universal archetypes within the collective unconscious. [*Volcanoes and the Subconscious Mind*]

Epilogue

Mountains are a wonderful metaphor for the challenges we encounter in life, and for the way we meet them. They are also a metaphor for the many opportunities and possibilities that come our way, and for the way we take advantage of them. When we climb mountains, we sometimes have to face our deepest fears and find ways of overcoming them. In doing so, we get to know ourselves, but we also learn more about our potential – what we could do, if we really put our mind to it. A spiritual quest is often described as mountainous journey.

> On mountains, we have to learn new skills and new knowledge, to be able to move safely and enjoyable. For example, we have to learn to 'read the terrain', just as we have to be able to understand what's happening in the world around us. And we have to learn to cooperate with, and trust, others, because on the mountains our lives sometimes depend on it. On mountains, we see 'new horizons' and 'new summits', and we are able to look at the world from 'new viewpoints', enabling to see completely new things or to understand things as we have never understood them before. [BodyMind Institute]

But it's not just a spiritual element that is influenced by the close proximity of these magical uplands. As I observed in *CRONE!*, I find living in close proximity to the mountains certainly generates creative energy, which might go a long way in explaining why, in the ten years I've lived here, I've managed to complete nearly thirty books in quick succession; several of which had been lying dormant for several years, not to mention the first in a series of esoteric novels.

By contrast, the time between living in Wales and Ireland,

was spent in the flat, reclaimed lands of Suffolk and rural Leicestershire, and produced hardly anything at all of a creative nature. On the western side of this central plain, the magical Malvern Hills are unlike any other outcrop in England and Wales, and may represent a slice of pre-Cambrian base-rock, which is only found at the surface in north-west Scotland. Weekends spent in the Malverns, however, also produced a surge of creative energy that quickly diminished after returning home on the plain. The Suffolk sojourn produced absolutely nothing at all, to the point of atrophy.

As I've observed before, the energies of the Glen are 'dark' – not in any negative sense – but because the primitive history of the place is unchanged and unchanging. And if, like me, you are someone who is attuned to primitive energies, then the magical/creative urges will be stimulated with a vengeance when living in such a magnificent location. But before you respond that this 'creative stimulus' is merely wishful thinking on the part of the writer, I would have to add that I experienced similar literary outpourings when living in my homeland of Wales, near the Preseli Mountains. Those slopes are also dotted with prehistoric remains, including evidence of Neolithic settlement and as I commented earlier in the text, they remain the same as when our ancient ancestors deemed them sacred. I am able to look at exactly the same landscape as they did thousands of years ago.

These mountains have their own blend of magic and mysticism – or as a farming neighbour often comments when we stand together and watch the changing colour and light moving across the slopes: "It makes you feel good with yourself, doesn't it?"

Sources & Bibliography

Axis of Heaven, Paul Broadhurst and Gabtiele Trso (Mythos)

Britain's Oldest Art: The Ice Age cave art of Creswell Crags, Paul Bahn and Paul Pettitt [Historic England]

Cave Art: A Guide to the Decorated Ice Age Caves of Europe: Paul Bahn (Frances Lincoln)

Confessions, Aleister Crowley (Arkana)

Creating Pre-History, Adam Stout (Blackwell)

The Crust of Our Earth, Chet Raymo (Phalarope Books)

Earth, James F Luhr (D&K)

The Elements of Earth Mysteries, Philip Heselton (Capall Bann)

The Great Goddess Re-discovered, Frater M (*Lamp of Thoth* magazine)

A History of Art, H W Jansen (Thames & Hudson)

Honey from Stone, Chet Raymo (Brandon)

A Phenomenology of Landscape, Christopher Tilley (Berg)

The Power of the Bull, Michael Rice (Routledge)

Shugendo: The Way of the Mountain Monks, Shokai Koshikidake (Faulks Books)

Starchild I & II, Melusine Draco (ignotus)

Traditional Witchcraft and the Path to the Mysteries, Melusine Draco (Moon Books) *The Tragic Human Condition,* Carl Gustav Jung and Miguel de Unamuno', Dr Ilse Vickers (Harvest)

Volcanoes and the Unconscious Mind: A Case Study, Justine Ariel (Brown University)

Bradshaw Foundation articles:
http://www.bradshawfoundation.com/lascaux/index.php

http://www.bradshawfoundation.com/chauvet/index.php

http://www.bradshawfoundation.com/cave_art_an_intuition_ of_eternity/decent_into_the_cave/shamanistic_visionary_ experience.php

http://www.bradshawfoundation.com/cave_art_an_intuition_
of_eternity/decent_into_the_cave/spring_initiation_rites_
homo_religioso.php

http://www.bradshawfoundation.com/malta/index.php

http://www.bradshawfoundation.com/british_isles_prehistory_
archive/gower_peninsula_south_wales/index.php

**MOON
BOOKS**

PAGANISM & SHAMANISM

What is Paganism? A religion, a spirituality, an alternative
belief system, nature worship? You can find support for all these
definitions (and many more) in dictionaries, encyclopaedias, and
text books of religion, but subscribe to any one and the truth will
evade you. Above all Paganism is a creative pursuit, an encounter
with reality, an exploration of meaning and an expression of the
soul. Druids, Heathens, Wiccans and others, all contribute their
insights and literary riches to the Pagan tradition. Moon Books
invites you to begin or to deepen your own encounter, right here,
right now.
If you have enjoyed this book, why not tell other readers by
posting a review on your preferred book site.

Medicine for the Soul
The Complete Book of Shamanic Healing
Ross Heaven
All you will ever need to know about shamanic healing and how to
become your own shaman…
Paperback: 978-1-78099-419-2 ebook: 978-1-78099-420-8

Shaman Pathways – The Druid Shaman
Exploring the Celtic Otherworld
Danu Forest
A practical guide to Celtic shamanism with exercises and
techniques as well as traditional lore for exploring the Celtic
Otherworld.
Paperback: 978-1-78099-615-8 ebook: 978-1-78099-616-5

Traditional Witchcraft for the Woods and Forests
A Witch's Guide to the Woodland with Guided Meditations and
Pathworking
Mélusine Draco
A Witch's guide to walking alone in the woods, with guided
meditations and pathworking.
Paperback: 978-1-84694-803-9 ebook: 978-1-84694-804-6

Wild Earth, Wild Soul
A Manual for an Ecstatic Culture
Bill Pfeiffer
Imagine a nature-based culture so alive and so connected,
spreading like wildfire. This book is the first flame…
Paperback: 978-1-78099-187-0 ebook: 978-1-78099-188-7

Naming the Goddess
Trevor Greenfield
Naming the Goddess is written by over eighty adherents and
scholars of Goddess and Goddess Spirituality.
Paperback: 978-1-78279-476-9 ebook: 978-1-78279-475-2

Shapeshifting into Higher Consciousness
Heal and Transform Yourself and Our World with Ancient
Shamanic and Modern Methods
Llyn Roberts
Ancient and modern methods that you can use every day to
transform yourself and make a positive difference in the world.
Paperback: 978-1-84694-843-5 ebook: 978-1-84694-844-2

Readers of ebooks can buy or view any of these bestsellers by
clicking on the live link in the title. Most titles are published in
paperback and as an ebook. Paperbacks are available in traditional
bookshops. Both print and ebook formats are available online.

Find more titles and sign up to our readers' newsletter at
http://www.johnhuntpublishing.com/paganism
Follow us on Facebook at https://www.facebook.com/MoonBooks
and Twitter at https://twitter.com/MoonBooksJHP